CW01655143

Sales Leadership Success

The 'one golden rule' for guiding your team, plus 20 invaluable lessons to supercharge your sales performance.

Paul Umpleby

ISBN: 9798343636635

First Edition: October 2024

Printed in United Kingdom

Contents

INTRODUCTION

Welcome

Thank you for purchasing this book. Your support means the world to me, and I'm delighted to have the opportunity to guide you on a journey to unlock the full potential of your sales leadership. As we explore each section and lesson, I hope you find the insights and strategies valuable and transformative for your business.

Each lesson in this book has been carefully developed, drawing from my extensive experience of over 25 years in sales - 20 of which I've spent in sales leadership roles. Throughout these pages, I'll share stories that illustrate the concepts, making them relatable and easier to implement. I'll also reveal the secrets to success for each lesson, along with the common pitfalls to watch out for, ensuring you can navigate your specific challenges with confidence.

My sincere wish is that you can take the knowledge and strategies from this book and apply them within your own business. By doing so, I hope you'll inspire your sales team to achieve even greater results, driving sustainable growth and success beyond what you're currently experiencing.

Why I Wrote This Book

After a successful corporate career leading sales teams and initiatives for some of the largest industrial manufacturing and distribution companies, I reached a crossroads. It had been a rewarding journey – and I had plenty to be thankful for. The corporate world provided a comfortable life for me and my family: my wife, Karen, who runs a holistic therapy and life coaching business, and our daughter, Harriet, who, at the time of writing, is studying her A-levels. We also have two Beagles, Poppy, and Ruby, who keep us 'entertained.'

Throughout my corporate journey, I've been fortunate to travel to over 25 countries, immerse myself in different cultures, and learn from some remarkable individuals. Along the way, I had the honour of being selected for and graduating from two prestigious senior leadership programmes, and I was sponsored through my MBA. I even had the support to relocate from Hartlepool in the North East of England to our current home in Peterborough, Cambridgeshire. The chance to help amazing businesses grow and to lead and coach some truly brilliant people has been deeply rewarding.

However, as someone who likes to give, it dawned on me that, as an employee, I could only give to one company at a time. I realised I had more to offer and that the corporate world, as fulfilling as it had been, was limiting my ability to help others. It became clear I needed a change.

That change came in November 2023, when I decided to start my own business, Bright Cube Consultancy. My goal was simple: to take everything I'd learnt from my corporate career and share it with businesses that may lack access to the strategies I had been fortunate enough to develop and refine over the years.

As I began building a framework for my consultancy, I noticed recurring lessons that had emerged throughout my career. When I started working with new clients, I quickly identified common patterns - missing pieces of the sales leadership puzzle that, when addressed, led to significant improvements. With each project, these lessons became clearer, and as I fine-tuned them, I realised that authoring this book was the natural next step.

By sharing my knowledge in this book, I hope to extend the impact of these lessons beyond my direct clients. All companies aiming to scale will undoubtedly benefit from many of the insights I've gathered throughout my corporate career. My hope is that these lessons will continue to develop within your business as you embark on your own sales leadership journey.

How To Use This Book

The book is structured into five sections: Business Development, Sales Management, Sales Development, Customer Engagement, and Continuous Improvement. Within each of the first four sections, you'll find five lessons, bringing us to a total of 20 lessons. The last section, the 'One Golden Rule' contains just one lesson that ties together everything you will have learned throughout the book.

I would be delighted if you could take something valuable from each lesson by reading the book in its entirety. However, if there are specific areas where you know you need to delve into the details, please feel free to jump straight into the relevant section. While you would benefit from absorbing all the lessons, you can still make progress by focusing on those that are most interesting or valuable to you.

My only request is that you do more than just read each section. Consider how each lesson can apply to your business. What strategies and tactics can you implement to help your business excel from where it currently stands? What actionable insights can you use to drive change? And how can you improve engagement with your sales team and your customers? However you choose to use this book, I hope you enjoy it.

Why Sales Leadership Matters

The term "sales leadership" is one I use to describe all facets of the people, processes, and systems that comprise your sales strategy. Each of these facets plays a crucial role in the overall success of your sales efforts.

People are at the heart of any business. They are the ones who build relationships with customers, understand their needs, and tailor solutions that meet those needs. The effectiveness of your sales team directly impacts your ability to generate revenue and grow your business. Skilled salespeople bring creativity, adaptability, and emotional intelligence to the table, which are critical for navigating complex sales cycles. Additionally, leadership within the sales team provides the right direction, motivation, and mentorship, ensuring that the entire team is aligned with the company's goals and strategies.

Processes provide the structure and the consistency necessary to manage and execute your sales activities effectively. When you have well-defined sales processes tailored to your business, they help standardise best practices, helping each team member to be self-sufficient and successful. This consistency enhances your business's efficiency and lays the foundation for more accurate forecasting and measurement of your sales performance. I've always found that clear processes are invaluable for recruitment, onboarding, and training, as they help new team members quickly adapt to your business and start contributing to your success. Perhaps most importantly, regularly reviewing these processes can help identify bottlenecks and areas for improvement, ensuring continuous optimisation of your entire sales function.

Systems is the enabler that brings your people and processes together as one. The right sales technology can significantly enhance your productivity by automating routine tasks, allowing salespeople to focus on higher-value activities. Customer Relationship Management (CRM) systems, for example, provide a centralised platform for managing customer interactions, tracking sales pipelines, and analysing data. Advanced analytics tools can offer insights into customer behaviour, which can help your sales teams make data-driven decisions. Furthermore, technology facilitates communication and collaboration within the sales team and across the organisation, breaking down any silos and ensuring that everyone is working towards the same goals and objectives.

Together, these facets making up people, processes, and systems, form the foundation of a robust sales leadership strategy. When each element is optimised and aligned, they create a powerful constructive collaboration that can drive your sales performance, enhance customer satisfaction, and deliver significant business growth. By paying attention to each of these facets, you can ensure that your sales strategy is always effective.

I'd like to wish you every success in your own sales leadership journey. I hope the insights and strategies you gain help you achieve your goals and drive your business to new levels of success.

BUSINESS DEVELOPMENT

Lesson 1: Marketing Alignment

I know what you're thinking. This was meant to be a book about sales leadership, wasn't it? So, why are we starting with marketing? In the 80s and 90s, sales were indeed the predominant driving force of the commercial function. New gurus were developing the latest methodologies to help salespeople structure and execute the perfect sales cycle. I remember my first field sales role in 2001. At that time, marketing activity was limited to creating content such as leaflets, guides, and flyers. It's probably why the boot of my Vauxhall Vectra, the standard rep's car of its day, never had any space for my personal belongings. It was constantly full of marketing material.

As my career developed, I saw new growth strategies emerging from the sales function. Each year brought a new focus aimed at growing sales, retaining clients, and improving profitability. In truth, there weren't many differences year to year - just a rework of the same strategies and tactics, regurgitated into a new format. There would be an annual sales kick-off, which was, in reality, the same as last year's sales kick-off. In my mind, I never found inspiration from these events.

The reason for this stagnation, I believe, lies in a role that persists even today: the Sales and Marketing Director. The very title implies that sales take precedence over marketing, but that couldn't be further from the truth. For any business aiming for greatness where these two roles are combined under one person, it should be titled Marketing and Sales Director. And if the company is large enough to justify having two senior leaders - a Sales Director and a Marketing Director - I believe that the Sales Director should always take strategic direction from the Marketing Director, with the Sales Director then being responsible for the execution of that strategy.

The Turning Tide

I saw this firsthand when I began working in my first big company as a salesperson in 2003. For the first year or two, I didn't have much exposure to the inner workings of strategic development. But gradually, I began to be exposed to more insights and noticed a trend: the marketing team set the strategy, and the sales team executed it. So much so that there seemed to be a fresh marketing hire every week. New roles were being developed, novel words were entering our vocabulary, and I began to see a shift where the marketing team became the real driving force behind the go-to-market plan for the business.

I attended the annual conference in 2005, and the opening session was led by the Marketing Director. The work the team had done to generate insights into the state of the market absolutely blew me away. They had turned over every stone to understand what needed to change in the business to generate significant growth. A structure was used that resonated with me then, and I still use it today:

Where are we now?

Where do we want to get to?

How are we going to get there?

It's simple, easy to understand, and hugely effective. That conference opened my eyes to what could be achieved by a marketing-led organisation. In other companies, I recalled poorly assembled slides crammed with clip art, but here, I witnessed a slick, highly polished, and convincing strategy presentation that everyone could rally behind. I'd often heard people dismiss marketing in the past with comments like, "They just colour things in, don't they?" But this was a stark contrast. The marketing team were clearly the architects of the five-year strategic plan to transform and accelerate the business. In fact, seeing that strategic shift from sales to marketing in just one morning cemented this power shift in my mind instantly.

Marketing Leadership

This marketing ownership continued to flourish, and I witnessed the formation of collaborative groups and meetings, all driven by a marketing-first approach. In each market segment, detailed strategic plans were created by marketing specialists, meaning the sales leadership team could focus on building the resources, skills, and knowledge needed to execute these plans. By this point, my mind was made up: if you wanted to succeed in sales, you had to work in close partnership with marketing and ensure they played a significant role in developing the business strategy.

Based on my previous experience, marketing had shifted from being merely a support function to a leading force within the organisation. This transformation didn't happen overnight - the trust had to be earned. But as more insights were gathered, I saw marketing gradually taking on greater responsibilities and becoming integral to decision-making processes. Marketing teams became the main source of intelligence, using data analytics and customer feedback to shape business strategies.

As marketing's influence grew, we in the sales team began to rely heavily on the insights and strategies developed by market vertical experts. This collaboration ensured that both departments were aligned on objectives, allowing the business as a whole to respond more effectively to customer needs and any market changes.

Marketing Insight Strategies

The shift in focus towards marketing was driven by the realisation that understanding the market and the customer was crucial to our overall success. Marketing teams were tasked with gathering data, analysing trends, and identifying opportunities for growth. They became the architects of business strategies, designing plans that were both data-driven and customer-focused.

These marketing insights played a pivotal role in shaping the sales strategies. By understanding customer needs, preferences, and behaviours, marketing teams could tailor their campaigns to reach the right audience with the right message. This targeted approach increased the likelihood of converting leads into sales and ensured that the business was meeting the needs of its customers.

The collaboration between sales and marketing also meant that sales teams were better prepared to engage with customers. Armed with insights from marketing, salespeople could have more informed conversations with customers, addressing their pain points and offering solutions that met their needs. We'll revisit the term "pain points" later in the book, but for now, here's a quick definition: A customer pain point is a specific problem, need, or frustration that gets in the way of their business objectives.

I consider myself genuinely fortunate to have learned so much during that time. Since those days, everything I've approached has always started with a marketing strategy at the core of everything we did moving forward.

Aligning Marketing and Sales Teams

Now that I've set the scene on why marketing is so crucial to the growth of any sales strategy, let's turn our attention to how the sales team needs to integrate with that growth plan and ensure there is no misalignment.

First things first. If there is a separate Sales Director and Marketing Director, they must tread the same path every day. I would even recommend a weekly meeting to provide feedback on strategy progress and ensure continuous improvement is central to the day-to-day operations. It starts at the top, and if the sales team thinks for one moment there is misalignment between the senior leaders, the strategy will fall at the first hurdle. These leaders must practice what they preach and show their respective teams that this is a team effort; one cannot succeed without the other. The sooner the leadership group gets aligned, the sooner the team can get to work.

With the rise in digital, it's common now that a customer will have researched your product or service, interacted with some content, and may have even seen a demo or information from a video. They will see what the sales team thinks about their own business from their LinkedIn posts and are more than capable of seeking out referrals from customers who have also used your service. Therefore, the sales team needs to be prepared to meet the customer wherever they are on that journey. It's important that they receive insights from marketing on the interactions that have already taken place with the customer prior to any engagement with sales. This helps speed up the sales cycle because the salesperson is better armed with information that can help them solve the customer's problem. The customer journey needs to be lock-stepped between both sales and marketing. The first time the customer sees any kind of misalignment, they will be on the phone to your competitors.

Qualified Marketing Leads

If you are fortunate, the marketing team will be delivering the strategy at the highest level. They'll be engaging both prospects and customers with lead-generation tactics that help convert interactions into marketing-qualified leads. For a salesperson, having a continual flow of marketing-qualified leads is a real joy, especially when they result in entry to the opportunity pipeline. One of the biggest complaints I've heard from sales teams over the years is this: "The marketing leads are a waste of time; I don't really bother with them." Just writing that down now makes the hairs on the back of my neck stand up. It's such a wasted opportunity for any salesperson.

Instead, you should encourage your sales team to interact with marketing to continually improve the quality of leads they are generating. Marketing, if they're lucky, might get to talk with customers when developing new strategies. A salesperson, however, is having conversations every day of the week. They have so many opportunities to have their finger on the pulse of the customers' problem areas. It's these problem areas that can be translated into marketing tactics. And guess what? If one customer is feeling it, you can bet many others are too.

That's the beauty of harmonising sales and marketing activity. The sales team can constantly gather customer insights that will feed the marketing team with innovative ideas, new strategies, and new goals. Remember earlier when I mentioned that there should be a weekly meeting between the sales and marketing leaders? Well, I couldn't think of a better time to provide feedback on market intelligence. A weekly flow of continuous improvement ideas to the marketing team is not just a silver bullet; it's a silver bullet machine. It's really that simple. Ensure your sales team is the voice of the customers. They should immerse themselves in the world in which their customers live, and the magic will begin to happen.

A small number of carefully targeted questions can open up endless possibilities of pain points that need to be addressed. These questions don't need to be complex. They need to be quite simple, easy-to-understand questions that just get the customer to think a little more deeply than the general day-to-day business noise that goes on around them. I'll provide further insights into these questions when we cover Lead Generation in Lesson 3.

If you have good rapport and have already delivered value to them, they are much more likely to open up. Remember, people open up to those that they know and trust. If, as a sales and marketing team, you can get this right, then there should be a continual stream of marketing-qualified leads, ready for conversion to sales-qualified leads, and on to the opportunity pipeline for sales closure.

Building a Collaborative Culture

To ensure that sales and marketing teams work together effectively, it's essential to build a culture of collaboration. This involves breaking down silos and encouraging open communication between departments. Those regular weekly meetings between the sales and marketing leaders will be critical. And regular brainstorming sessions can help teams align their goals and continuously develop strategies.

Ownership and accountability are key. Both the sales and marketing teams should see themselves as partners working towards a common goal: driving business growth and delivering exceptional value to customers. It's crucial for the leadership team to recognise and celebrate successes along the way. Acknowledging the contributions of both teams will strengthen their bond and reinforce the importance of their ongoing collaboration. When everyone feels valued and appreciated, they are more likely to go the extra mile for the business.

Reimagined Leadership Roles

If you are fortunate enough to work in a business that has the luxury of separate sales and marketing leadership, you must embrace it all that you can to ensure the sales team is fully aligned with the marketing team and their strategies. Develop together, learn from each other, and never stop improving.

For those Sales and Marketing Directors reading, I seriously want you to consider the benefits of flipping your role to become a Marketing and Sales Director. Start with a marketing strategy and build your team to execute that strategy. By prioritising marketing and allowing it to guide the sales function, I believe you will unlock new levels of success across the business.

Conclusion

The shift from sales to marketing as the driving force behind your business strategy should be seen as a positive development. By recognising the importance of marketing insights and aligning the sales and marketing effort, I'm confident you can create a cohesive and effective approach to your growth plan. Ultimately, the key to success lies in recognising the value of both sales and marketing and understanding how they can complement each other to achieve the overarching business goals and objectives. Embrace the power of collaboration and start working together as one unified team.

Lesson 2: Value Proposition

If you've reached this lesson, thank you, and I hope you are enjoying what you've learned so far. Our exploration of marketing alignment in the previous lesson was the first step toward creating a value proposition. It's crucial to grasp how marketing functions can be a driving force for your business, setting your go-to-market strategy. The core strategies developed in your marketing plan should be the cornerstone of your value proposition. By now, you should have a clear idea of what makes your company unique in the eyes of your customers. In this lesson, we'll dive deeper into how to create a compelling value proposition and the impact it can have on your business.

Understanding the Value Proposition

A company's value proposition links its purpose to the real value it offers customers. It explains how the company's products or services solve customer problems and meet their needs. By highlighting unique benefits, the value proposition shows how the company's purpose aligns with customer priorities, building trust and delivering meaningful results.

Therefore, a value proposition is more than just a brief sales statement – it's the heart of your strategy and the essence of what your company stands for. It explains the value and benefits a product, or service offers to a target audience. Your value proposition should highlight the problem your solution solves, the advantages it provides, and why it's better than competitors. A strong value proposition isn't just a slogan; I believe it should be a promise to your customers.

Here are three critical elements to consider:

Specific: What are the exact benefits the target customer will receive? Being specific helps in differentiating your product from others. For example, if your product saves customers time, how much time are they saving, and what does that time equate to in terms of value?

Pain-focused: How will your product or service solve the customer's problem or improve their life? Customers are looking for solutions that directly address their pain points. Whether it's reducing costs, improving efficiency, or simply making things more convenient, your value proposition should speak directly to these issues.

Exclusive: How is your product or service both desirable and unique? How well does it highlight the company's competitive advantage and set it apart from competitors? Exclusivity doesn't necessarily mean rarity; it means positioning your offer in a way that makes customers feel they are getting something they can't easily find elsewhere.

Creating a compelling value proposition requires a deep understanding of your customers business and of course, the market landscape. It's a strategic element that looks outward at customers and the demand side of the business. Finding a unique value proposition allows you to tap into previously unaddressed customer needs. This, in turn, can help you expand your market reach.

Value Proposition Essentials

Your value proposition should be a strategic asset that impacts every aspect of your business. It influences how your marketing team positions your products, how your brand is perceived in the market, and then how your sales teams communicate with your customers. It should serve as the foundation for all your marketing efforts. It ensures consistency across all channels – from your website to your email campaigns, to your social media presence. This consistency helps to build trust with your customers, as they know exactly what to expect from your brand.

Most importantly, a clear value proposition simplifies the decision-making process for your customers. In a world where consumers are overwhelmed with choices, a compelling value proposition cuts through the noise and helps them quickly understand why they should choose your product or service over others.

My Lived Experience

One of my favourite examples of a company with a strong value proposition that has made my life easier on numerous occasions is Uber. During my time in corporate roles, I often found myself arriving in unfamiliar airports and cities at odd hours of the day and night. I'm sure you've experienced it too: you follow the signs for the exit, hoping to see something familiar at the taxi rank. You walk up, bags in hand, tired and simply wanting to get to your hotel. You find a taxi at the front of the line, only to discover it's a small Toyota Aygo with barely enough legroom. What's more disappointing is the gleaming Mercedes E-Class AMG next in line, which you're not allowed to take because you must take the front one.

You get in, try to explain to the driver where you'd like to go, and, in typical British fashion, realise you don't know a single word in the local language. You fumble with your phone, trying to find the address, and the driver reads it while driving (quite dangerous I always find). Then comes the decisive moment: "You do take credit cards, don't you?" If they do, you're relieved, but the next worry sets in: "How much is this going to cost?" Watching the meter tick over without any clue of the final fare, you can't help but feel uneasy. Finally, you arrive, you pay with your card, and the driver scribbles a receipt on the back of a business card and throws it over his shoulder at you. The entire experience leaves you stressed and frustrated.

Contrast that with my first experience using Uber. It was at Paris Charles de Gaulle Airport. I was heading to a training session in Collégien, not far from Disneyland Paris. A colleague had recommended downloading the app before I travelled, as Uber had a large network around the city and would be great for short transfers and airport journeys. Before travelling, I tested the app and saw that several cars were available around the airport. I could see the fee, which would automatically be charged to my credit card. This small practice run before the trip significantly eased the tension I usually felt upon arrival.

When I arrived, I picked up my suitcase, stood near the exit, and requested a trip. The app instantly gave me the car's registration number, make and model, and told me where to wait. Two minutes later, I was in the car. The driver knew exactly where to go, I knew the route, the estimated arrival time, and the fee, and at the end of the trip, I received a digital receipt on my phone.

This experience perfectly depicts Uber's value proposition: removing all the tension from the journey, making me feel relaxed, in control, and knowledgeable about what lay ahead. For someone who travelled frequently for work, that feeling was priceless. Uber didn't just provide a service – it provided peace of mind. And that, in essence, is what a strong value proposition should do: offer something invaluable to the customer beyond the basic product or service.

Uber's Value Proposition

My interpretation of Uber's value proposition is to provide a simple, convenient, and affordable transportation service through their app. Their service is considered to be better than traditional taxis, which can be unreliable and may have unclear pricing. Uber's value proposition includes:

Convenience: Uber's app allows customers to request a car with one tap, track their driver's location in real-time, and make cashless payments. Uber cars are generally available 24/7, offering a level of reliability that traditional taxis may struggle to match.

Affordability: Uber fares are generally cheaper than taxis, although I wouldn't mind paying slightly more for the convenience factor. The transparency in pricing also eliminates the anxiety of unexpected costs, something traditional taxis may fail to provide.

Reliability: Uber aims to provide a reliable service. You know what to expect, how long it will take to arrive at your destination, and what the journey will cost. The ability to rate drivers and provide feedback also ensures that service quality is consistently high.

As a progressive company, Uber's core messaging has evolved over the years as it grows and expands. At the time of writing, the Uber website stated:

"We reimagine the way the world moves for the better. Movement is what we power. It's our lifeblood. It runs through our veins. It's what gets us out of bed each morning.

It pushes us to constantly reimagine how we can move better. For you. For all the places you want to go. For all the things you want to get. For all the ways you want to earn. Across the entire world. In real-time. At the incredible speed of now."

Now, that sounds grander than just wanting a quick taxi ride from the airport, but you can see the essence of the message they're trying to deliver. All The Places, All The Things, All The Ways. Yes, I can resonate with that.

This evolution of Uber's messaging reflects the company's ambitions to not just be a transportation provider, but a platform that empowers movement in all forms – whether that's people, goods, or even opportunities. This shift in value proposition shows the importance of adaptability. As markets evolve and customer expectations change, so too must your value proposition.

Value Propositions in Manufacturing

Let's explore a different value proposition by delving into real-life insights on how customer communication can be entirely centred on the value you deliver, setting you apart from the competition. I'll draw on my experience with a manufacturing company.

This business, let's call it **Sun**, manufactured a product that many other manufacturers also made. There were (and still are) lots of competitors vying for market share. However, in reality, there were two other main players with similar scale and breadth of offerings: **Moon** and **Star**.

All three businesses were well-respected, known for their high-quality products, and employed the absolute best people in their field. In fact, it was common for employees to move between these three businesses to advance their careers. This was welcomed because if someone came from one of these competitors, they were always exceptionally talented.

During a strategic market review at **Sun**, we aimed to redefine our value proposition – the thing that made us unique. In this market, there were three primary areas where you could be "famous": **Technology**, **Price**, or **Service**.

Moon was a thought leader in the market. Each year, they spent considerably more on research and development than their direct competitors. They invested in displaying innovative, forward-thinking insights, demonstrating where the market was headed in three or even five years. If you were a customer looking for the latest and greatest **Technology**, **Moon** was your choice.

Star focused on high-volume production at a lower cost. They invested in state-of-the-art manufacturing facilities and consolidated their operations, allowing them to serve the global market efficiently. Their strategy was centred around offering a more reasonable **Price** option without sacrificing quality, making them the preferred choice for customers looking for large volumes of standard products.

This left space for **Sun** to position itself as the **Service** leader. **Sun** specialised in value engineering, working with customers to refine products to meet exact specifications. With centres of excellence worldwide, staffed by highly skilled engineers, **Sun** solved complex customer challenges through customised solutions.

Sun communicated this value proposition clearly and consistently. Every marketing message emphasised their focus on **Service**. Customers knew what to expect: a company that would go beyond to solve their biggest challenges. Whether it was a new product development or a challenging technical requirement, they were the go-to partner for engineering excellence. This clarity in communication not only helped attract new customers but also solidified relationships with existing ones.

The company also made sure to invest in training its sales and customer service teams. They were not just selling a product; they were selling a solution, a partnership. This approach significantly reduced churn rates and increased customer loyalty. In a market where switching suppliers was common, it managed to retain customers by consistently delivering on its value proposition.

Executing the Value Proposition

Let's not forget that this is a book about Sales Leadership. So, what does this value proposition mean for the sales team, who are tasked with executing the strategy directly with customers?

It couldn't be easier. Everywhere the customer looked – whether on the website, in trade publications, via email marketing, or on LinkedIn – the messages were the same: **We are the Service leader**. For the sales team, this clarity made their job straightforward. They simply needed to relay and act upon those messages when talking with customers and prospects. A clear value proposition simplifies the sales process by eliminating ambiguity. When your sales team knows exactly what value they're offering, they can focus on building brilliant relationships and solving complex problems.

This goes back to Marketing Alignment, as discussed in Lesson 1. If your sales team is fully aligned with your marketing team, you'll have a clear go-to-market plan and a well-defined value proposition. The sales team executes the value proposition by finding customers with the biggest pain points and solving those problems through expert engineering services. This ensures a win for the customer and the business. It's a simple formula that keeps the sales team moving in the same direction.

In addition to being a forward-looking strategy, a well-executed value proposition also empowers your sales team to handle any objections more effectively. When customers express doubts or concerns, a strong value proposition allows your sales team to confidently address them by reinforcing those unique benefits your product or service offers.

Conclusion

A well-defined value proposition should be the guiding principle that aligns your entire business; call it the **North Star**. Whether you're a service-oriented company or a manufacturing giant, knowing what you want to be famous for and communicating that message clearly is essential to your success. Your value proposition is the promise you make to your customers, and when executed well, it can transform your business. As you continue to refine your own value proposition, remember to stay aligned with your core strategies, communicate your strengths consistently, and always keep the customer at the centre of your messaging.

Lesson 3: Lead Generation

Now that we have good alignment between the marketing and sales teams, along with a clear value proposition across the business, it's time to turn our attention to the first step in the sales cycle: lead generation. However, before diving into tactics, it's important to truly understand what lead generation is, who is responsible for it, and how to maximise its benefits.

Lead generation is the process of identifying and attracting potential customers who have shown interest in your product or service. It's about building a pipeline of prospects who can eventually convert into paying customers. While this might sound straightforward, it involves a strategic mix of marketing and sales efforts and requires constant evaluation and adjustment.

Armed with your value proposition, lead generation should feel like a natural next step. You've already done the hard work – you know what your business stands for and what sets it apart from the competition. Now, it's about communicating that effectively to your target audience. But remember, it's not just about sending out tons of emails and hoping the leads will come flooding in. Success in lead generation often requires trying different approaches, learning from what works, what doesn't, and being willing to adapt as you go. The key lies in targeting your communication efforts based on the unique needs of each segment of your audience.

Understanding the Market

To understand the importance of tailoring your approach, let's look at an example where a company serves both machine builders and maintenance engineers with the same product. Differentiation is crucial when addressing multiple markets, so let's have some fun with a fictional example. One of my favourite movies of all time is *Back to the Future*. If you've seen it, you'll remember the Flux Capacitor in the DeLorean Time Machine. Imagine we're selling Flux Capacitors to a broad spectrum of DeLorean Time Machine builders – yes, imagine if there were more than one!

These machine builders are continuously looking for ways to make their products more efficient, effective, and less prone to error. Factors such as size, weight, and material type might be critical attributes they focus on. In a competitive market, cost becomes vital to survival, and in nearly every scenario, they will likely have one eye firmly focused on continuous improvement. As a supplier, if you want your component to be noticed, you need to ensure that your lead generation tactics highlight the value you bring to these areas. If your messaging doesn't resonate with their specific needs, your efforts may go unnoticed.

In our Flux Capacitor example, what else might be important to the machine builder? My guess is that accuracy and repeatability would top the list. Weight and physical size would also be significant considerations – after all, the cockpit of a DeLorean looks tight. They might also be interested in how your product can help them reduce manufacturing costs or improve the reliability of their time machines. If you can demonstrate this through your lead generation efforts, you're more likely to capture their attention.

Differentiating the Market

Now, let's shift our focus to another potential user of the Flux Capacitor: a maintenance engineer. This engineer's primary concern is ensuring that the Time Machine they maintain runs at its optimum potential. Their needs are different from those of the machine builder, and so too must be your lead generation approach.

For the maintenance engineer, the focus isn't on the design or manufacturing process but on the reliability and availability of replacement parts. When a Time Machine breaks down, they need parts quickly to get it back in working order. In this case, price may not be the most crucial factor; instead, availability, speed of delivery, and quality of packaging are key. If your lead generation strategy emphasises this, you're more likely to win their business.

This example illustrates a fundamental truth about lead generation: the same product can have vastly different appeal depending on the user. Understanding the specific needs of your target audience and tailoring your approach accordingly is critical to generating effective leads. This approach ensures that your messaging resonates with the right people, at the right time, in the right way.

Product vs. Service Approaches

To further explore the importance of segmentation in lead generation, let's look at a service-based business model. Holidays are something I'm passionate about, and over the years, I've travelled with many different travel companies. As a result, my inbox is often flooded with emails offering the latest destinations and deals. These companies know me well – after all, I've booked with them before, so they can segment me into a specific demographic.

When I was younger, holidays were all about the party atmosphere. How could I get the most fun, the least amount of sleep, and all for the lowest possible cost? If I were still in that demographic today, I'd be inundated with emails and social media adverts promising beach parties, boat trips, and limitless cocktails. And honestly, I'd probably welcome this targeting because it would help me quickly assess whether a particular holiday suited my interests.

As I matured, married my wife, and we had our daughter, our holiday priorities shifted. The hotels we stayed in needed to be more comfortable, with great facilities and a variety of food options. It was no longer just about my individual needs; I wanted to ensure we all had a brilliant time. This meant that family entertainment, fabulous pools, and – you guessed it – limitless cocktails became the focus of the holiday communications that appealed to me.

Today, our daughter is grown up and shares our appreciation for healthy food. Our overseas holidays are less frequent now, especially since we have our two crazy dogs, and prefer UK-based adventures. But when we do search for sun, our expectations are high. We now look for luxury, and with vegan diets, our holiday choices must cater to those needs while still offering a high-quality experience. For holiday companies targeting me today, I want to see luxurious rooms, lavish plant-based food choices, and, of course, those limitless cocktails.

This example demonstrates how, over time, the same customer can have vastly diverse needs. A one-size-fits-all approach won't work – companies need to understand and adapt to the evolving desires of their customers. Whether you're selling a product like the Flux Capacitor or a service like holidays, segmentation is key to lead generation.

The Lead Generation Process

Marketing plays a crucial role in developing lead generation strategies and tactics. This process follows on from the work done in the marketing plan, shifting from strategic planning to actionable tactics that can help generate new and recurring business with both prospects and customers. Effective lead generation requires a deep understanding of your target audience, prominent levels of customer insight, and a dash of creativity.

Gone are the days when a single marketing activity could drive lead generation. Today, it's about creating a comprehensive, multi-channel strategy that engages your audience wherever they are. If you're a social media user like me, you're likely familiar with paid advertising and remarketing techniques that ensure you see the same messages across various platforms. It can feel like these ads are following you around, but that's precisely the point.

Multi-Channel Lead Generation

Let's look at an example of how a multi-channel approach to lead generation might work in practice. Imagine you're a company owner interested in reducing energy bills by installing solar panels and insulating your building. You start with a Google search, which presents several paid ads alongside organic results. One ad catches your eye, so you click to find out more. The site asks for your email to download an energy-saving guide, but you decide not to at this stage and leave the page because you have a meeting.

Later that evening, while browsing Facebook, you see an ad for the same energy company. There's a call-to-action button asking if you'd like to download the guide, but you're busy watching *MasterChef*. The next morning, you check

LinkedIn and again see a sponsored ad for the same company. Finally, you decide to download the guide but plan to read it later. By 4 pm, with a cup of tea in hand, you review the guide, and just as you start reading, your phone pings – it's an email from the same energy company, with an impactful headline, clear benefits, and great testimonials.

In less than 24 hours, this energy company's lead generation tactics have you filling in a contact form, arranging a consultation. Success! This example highlights how multiple touchpoints across different channels can work together to nurture a lead from initial interest to conversion. It's not just about being persistent; it's about being present wherever your potential customers are and providing them with valuable content at each stage of their journey.

Sales and Marketing Teamwork

We've discussed a lot about marketing, and now it's time to bring our sales operations mindset to the forefront as we work out the role the sales team plays in the lead generation strategy. In my experience, the biggest cause of conflict between marketing and sales often centres around leads. The marketing team frequently complains that sales fail to follow up on leads, while the sales team argues that the leads are of inferior quality. This back-and-forth can lead to a stalemate, with both sides hoping that at least some of the leads will convert into quality opportunities.

Manage Your Lead Quality

My approach to resolving this conflict is straightforward. Whenever I hear complaints from the sales team about lead quality, I ask them a simple question: what steps have you taken to improve the quality of the leads you receive? This question shifts the responsibility back to the sales team and encourages them to work collaboratively with marketing to improve the lead generation process.

Returning to the theme of marketing alignment, it's essential that the marketing and sales teams fully support one another. If the marketing team has developed the strategic plan and created the value proposition, it makes perfect sense for them to lead the tactics that fill the pipeline with high-quality leads. Marketing should manage the process, the content, and the automation. However, the sales team plays a much bigger role than many salespeople understand.

Market conditions are constantly shifting, and so are customer requirements. The sales team is in the trenches every day, visiting customer premises, talking to employees, and hearing about new challenges as they arise. This gives sales a unique perspective on evolving customer needs and market dynamics, making their input invaluable to the lead generation process.

As a salesperson, it's essential to ask meaningful questions that keep you aligned with shifting market dynamics and allow you to adapt your lead generation strategies accordingly. While I'm not a big fan of "question banks" - they can often feel too scripted - I believe that when you're truly listening, the right questions tend to emerge naturally. It's a skill that comes with practice.

That said, I thought I'd share a few questions as a starting point, but I'm confident your sales team can easily adapt and refine them to better fit your specific industry with just a bit of focused effort. They could do this by analysing recent client interactions, reviewing common pain points, or discussing recurring themes during team meetings to ensure the questions address the issues your prospects face most often.

What challenges are you currently facing in your industry that weren't as prominent before?

- This question helps identify new pain points or emerging trends that may signal a shift in the market.

How have your priorities or goals changed in recent months?

- Understanding any changes in the customer's objectives can reveal shifts in market demands or opportunities.

What are your customers or end-users asking for now that they weren't before?

- This helps uncover evolving customer preferences or expectations, indicating market trends.

Are there any new competitors or market entrants that you're keeping an eye on?

- Gaining insights into the competitive landscape helps the salesperson anticipate market shifts and adjust their strategy accordingly.

How are you adapting your business strategies to current economic or industry trends?

- This question reveals how the customer is responding to external factors and can provide clues about broader market movements.

The answers to these questions (and others) can reveal a lot about how your marketing and sales efforts could evolve.

A Culture of Continuous Improvement

Assuming your sales team is generating regular insights (and I certainly hope they are), it's important to have a regular forum where marketing and sales come together to develop the lead generation plan. If you can build a culture of continuous improvement, the teams will naturally collaborate, as it's in their best interest to evolve the strategy to drive up the volume of high-quality leads, ready for conversion by the sales team.

These forums should be structured to encourage open dialogue, with both teams sharing their insights and challenges. This ongoing communication helps ensure that the lead generation strategy remains relevant and effective, adapting to changing market conditions and customer needs. As the strategy evolves, so too will the quality and quantity of leads, ultimately leading to better outcomes.

Conclusion

Lead generation works best when marketing <u>and</u> sales come together as one team. It's really about collaboration and ensuring everyone is aligned to the same goals. If you can take the time to understand the different market requirements and keep up with how they're evolving, I believe your business will have a much better chance of generating and converting high-quality leads effectively.

As we move forward, we'll be looking at how those leads, once ready for conversion, make their way into your opportunity pipeline. That's where we'll be focusing in our next lesson, exploring ways to make sure you're getting the most out of those opportunities.

Lesson 4: Opportunity Pipeline

Now that your marketing and sales teams are in perfect alignment, you've developed a compelling value proposition, and you're seeing a steady stream of warm leads, it's time to focus on the opportunity pipeline. For any business aiming for long-term success, having a strong, well-maintained pipeline with a continuous flow of new opportunities is crucial for future growth.

There are many ways to ensure your pipeline is effectively managed, and we'll dive into a few examples shortly. But before we do, I wanted to share some of the high-level approaches that resonate with me the most and have proven to be particularly impactful.

Prioritise High-Value Leads: It's important to focus your efforts where they'll have the most impact. By prioritising on your high-value leads, you will ensure that your team's time and resources are spent on opportunities with the best chance of converting. This helps you to make sure the right people are working on the leads that matter most, giving you the best chance of success.

Optimise Sales Processes: Streamlining your sales processes can really make a difference when it comes to closing deals more efficiently. By refining the end-to-end steps involved, you can help your team reduce the time it takes to bring opportunities over the line. This might mean simplifying systems, removing unnecessary steps, or identifying areas that slow things down. The goal is to make sure your team can work smoothly and consistently, without losing quality along the way.

Monitor Sales Performance: Keeping a keen eye on how things are going is key to knowing what's working and where adjustments might be needed. If you can use accurate data to guide your decisions, you will gain valuable insights and ensure your approach stays relevant and highly effective.

Improve Sales Efficiency: Salespeople need to use their time wisely, focusing on what's going to bring the most value to their customers and the business. By helping them prioritise their efforts and tailoring their approach to the value each customer brings, you can make sure they're spending their time where it counts. They have to work smarter, ensuring the right balance between quick wins and building longer-term relationships that could pay off further down the line.

Drive Sales Forecasting Accuracy: Keeping an accurate sales forecast can really help when it comes to planning for the future. By understanding what's likely to come, you can set clearer goals and prepare for the months and years ahead with confidence. Strong forecasting not only helps with the sales and operational planning but also makes sure everyone is working towards realistic, achievable targets.

Refine Sales Strategies: No strategy should ever stand still. Markets change, and it's important to keep adjusting your approach to stay relevant. If you can regularly review and refine your sales strategy, you will ensure it continues to align with your business goals and current market conditions. This continuous improvement helps you stay agile and competitive, always looking for ways to do things better across the team and to keep growing.

Nurturing Your Pipeline

For any salesperson, the pipeline is a critical aspect of their role, and they should care for it as if it were their own new-born baby. For context, I'm not talking about changing nappies when things go horribly wrong. What I mean is that, just like with a baby, you should never leave your pipeline alone – even for a brief period of time.

In those early days, you're constantly watching over your baby, checking that everything is okay, nurturing them, and ensuring everything is provided. As your baby grows into childhood, the nurturing continues, but you start to encourage, stretch, and even challenge your child to go that bit further for themselves. When I became a father, it altered my purpose. My role became about nurturing and developing my child to the best of my ability. You may find this comparison a bit extreme, but I believe that a salesperson should nurture and develop their pipeline with the same level of care and attention as they would with their baby or child.

Building a Strong Foundation

Getting control of your sales pipeline early in a sales role is crucial. A manager of mine used to say, "When you can boast about your sales, then boast about your sales. If sales aren't so good, then boast about your order book. If the order book is empty, then you'd better rely on a strong opportunity pipeline. And if your pipeline is rubbish, then you'd better have a strong story about the activities you're doing to fill it." Actually, he never used the term "rubbish," but I expect you can insert an appropriate word in its place.

This advice makes good sense. Activity today fills the pipeline tomorrow, and that pipeline contains all the golden nuggets of opportunity needed to secure orders and, eventually, sales.

My Pipeline Journey

I've managed a pipeline throughout my sales career, but my true understanding of how to drive and manage it REALLY WELL only came in my late 40s. As Regional Leader, my role was to find, nurture and develop new business. Unfortunately, when I started, the region had been vacant for some time. This meant many older opportunities had gone cold, and there was an extremely poor inflow of new opportunities. It almost felt like a start-up, where we had to begin with almost nothing, making activity levels in the first quarter vital.

Thankfully, I had the best sales lead generator I've ever met on the team. This guy had no fear, and once we had organised our ideal target customer, he relentlessly pursued opportunities. He confidently reached out to senior executives, creating personalised messages, and securing introductory conversations for me, showing an impressive ability to get straight to decision-makers with ease.

To help you understand and visualise what we were faced with, imagine a series of columns – left to right. When we started, all those columns were fairly empty. However, once the lead generations efforts kicked in, the left-hand column, showing companies that had booked an introductory call with us, began to fill up. As weeks passed, opportunities moved from one column to the next - discovery meetings, uncovering pain points, putting together proposals, and agreeing on terms. Finally, some opportunities reached the right-hand column - a win!

Pipeline Reviews and Learning

I recall the monthly and quarterly review meetings with my Vice President. He needed that right-hand win column to be full, and for us to reach targets. Since I couldn't talk about wins just yet, I was able to explain in detail what the biggest opportunities were and what the next steps would be. Additionally, I could articulate the activities we were doing across the team to ensure a continuous feed of new opportunities.

The opportunity pipeline became the only thing I needed each day. It was set as my home page for my CRM. Just like caring for a child, I would check in on the pipeline each morning, assess what development we could achieve that day, ensure nothing was going wrong, and confirm that everything was healthy. By the end of the day, I could rest and be proud, knowing we had made some great progress.

Applying My Learnings to Consultancy

I have much to be grateful for through those opportunity pipeline experiences. It helped me understand the value of managing an opportunity pipeline effectively and efficiently. This understanding has allowed me to establish a robust opportunity pipeline process for my consultancy business. I've also been able to share my insights and experiences with my consulting clients, adjusting and tailoring the processes to their specific business models and commercial requirements.

Establishing a Solid Pipeline Process

How do you set up a solid process for managing your opportunity pipeline? The first thing to keep in mind is that it should always reflect your current sales cycle and methodology. Your pipeline needs to align with how your team is actually working, ensuring everything moves smoothly through each stage.

I'll go into more detail when we get to Lesson 7, where we'll cover Selling Methodologies. We'll look at how misalignment between your training and processes can lead to wasted time, resources, and money - and how to avoid these issues. For now, though, let's keep things simple and say that the steps in the opportunity pipeline need to make sense - they must reflect what actually happens in your business day to day.

We should always start by putting the customer front and centre: what is the buying journey they are on, and how can we guide them through it effectively? Think about what they need to see, hear, and feel at each stage before they're ready to take the next step. Even the most skilled salespeople will struggle to close a deal if the customer isn't in sync with the process. That's why it's so important to create a clear alignment between the customer's buying journey and the stages your sales team is working through. When both sides are moving together, it's much easier to build trust, create momentum, and guide the customer towards a confident decision.

My Pipeline Process

To help bring this concept to life, let's take a look at the pipeline process for my consultancy business. It's broken down into seven steps, each designed to align closely with the customer's buying journey. By structuring the process this way, it helps ensure that I'm meeting the customer's needs at every stage, creating a seamless experience that supports their decision-making.

Steps	Buying Journey	Sales Process	Pipeline Status
1	Aware	Rapport	Initial Outreach
2	Learn	Discovery	Needs Assessed
3	Consider	Problems	Pain Known
4	Evaluate	Presentation	Solution Presented
5	Decide	Proposal	Proposal Submitted
6	Negotiate	Objections	Terms Finalised
7	Buy	Close	Won

As I mentioned, we will cover these steps in greater detail when we discuss Sales Methodologies later in the book, but for now, I'd like to explore the relationship between the buying journey and the sales process. I'll also provide some examples to help you identify when it's right - and when you've missed out on a vital component.

Let's focus on Step 2 and Step 5. I assume you understand Step 1, where the customer is hearing for the first time what your company does. It's important to build good rapport to move on to Step 2.

In my opinion, Step 2 is the most critical stage for all salespeople. However, many are too eager to move forward to the more exciting parts of the process, often presenting too soon, before the customer is on board with whether a partnership can exist. Always resist the urge to skip Step 2. Spend quality time allowing the customer to learn how well you listen and understand their business and its challenges.

Step 3 allows you to dig deeper into their problems, but at this most important stage (Step 2), a gentler approach is required. I believe a salesperson is being assessed in two key areas here:

Are You Really Listening? Does the potential customer feel you understand where they're coming from? Are you putting their needs before your own? Are you asking relevant questions because you genuinely want to help? If you fail to meet the buyer's expectations at this stage, the later stages will be, at best, a struggle and, at worst, a waste of time for everyone.

Do You Meet Their Expectations? Based on those early interactions, does the customer believe your solution will fulfil their requirements? They're not looking for absolute detail here, just enough to have confidence in continuing the conversation.

Your Assessment of The Customer

It's not all one-sided. As a salesperson, you should assess if there's a genuine opportunity here. Is the person you're speaking to able to progress the sale? Are they senior enough to decide? Who else needs to be involved? Do they have the budget? What are the timescales? What would success look like to them?

These questions, subtly woven into the conversation, should help you gauge whether it's worth investing more time. By using them naturally during your discussions, you can uncover key insights about the prospect's commitments.

Far too many opportunities progress to later stages when it was evident early on that the foundations weren't strong enough to build a partnership. I'll assume you felt confident enough to move to Step 4 and deliver a fantastic presentation. Now, let's progress on to Step 5.

Avoiding Missed Opportunities

At Step 5, the customer is making a near-final decision. You should know all their pain points, have presented your solution, and submitted your proposal. It's a great feeling when you send that proposal - it's the start of the end, if that makes sense. However, the issue arises when the salesperson didn't listen closely enough in the early stages. They missed uncovering the real pain points, failed to recognise all decision-makers, and didn't show up as the partner that can solve the problem. Consequently, you become just another vendor who spent hours, days, weeks, or even months of effort for nothing.

That's why each step, aligning the buying journey with the sales process, must be fully exhausted before moving on. Spending an extra thirty minute's building rapport at the start, or meeting more of the customer's colleagues during discovery, could make all the difference in the final phases.

Conclusion

Having a robust opportunity pipeline that you nurture and develop with care is vital for reaching your targets. There's a clear logic to the process: each stage plays a crucial role in building momentum, making the transition to the next step feel more natural and seamless. By the time you reach Step 7 of the process and ask for the order, your customer should feel completely confident that you are the right partner for their needs.

In our next lesson, we'll explore how to effectively develop pricing for your final solution and create a proposal that makes it easy for the customer to say yes. This preparation is essential, as it not only solidifies your position as a trusted partner but also ensures that the customer feels fully supported in their decision-making process.

Lesson 5: Pricing and Discounts

In this lesson on pricing and discounts, we'll focus on the execution of this crucial sales step rather than deep dive into price setting or price optimisation. These areas are specialised, and there are far more qualified experts who can guide you through them. One standout individual in the field of pricing strategy is Danilo Zatta, author of *The Pricing Model Revolution*. I've had the pleasure of reading his book and hearing him speak at a pricing conference, and I was blown away by both his knowledge and his ability to communicate complex concepts in simple, digestible terms.

Zatta's book explores how adopting innovative pricing models can help businesses gain a competitive edge. More importantly, it demonstrates the latest methods to monetise your products or services. I'd call it a pricing handbook - an essential read in your quest to improve your sales operation. Look him up if this is of interest!

Importance of Pricing in Profitability

Profitability is likely the number one priority in your business. After all, what's the point of running a company if you're not making money? You've probably tried everything to improve profits - selling more products, reducing expenditure, or cutting fixed costs. But here's something you may not have considered: price is the biggest lever you can pull to improve profitability.

Back in 2003, McKinsey released an article titled *The Power of Pricing*, which highlighted the profound impact that pricing can have on operating profits. According to their research, a 1% price increase can generate an 8% rise in operating profits - far outpacing the effects of cutting costs or increasing your sales volume. This is because pricing directly influences the bottom line without requiring any additional resources or investments.

Imagine this: you typically sell a product for £100. You change nothing in your business, but you increase the price to £101 - a mere 1% increase. That extra £1 goes straight to your bottom line as profit. It cost you no more to produce or sell the item, but the impact of that small price hike, when applied across your business, could be transformational.

McKinsey goes on to explain how effective pricing strategies can help businesses navigate market challenges. While cost-cutting opportunities are limited, and market growth can be unpredictable, optimising pricing - especially at the transaction level where your sales teams are active - can unlock hidden profitability. By refining your pricing tactics, you can aim to prevent revenue leakage from unnecessary discounts and incentives, maximising the value captured from each sale. We'll explore discounts in more detail later in this lesson, as they often represent the biggest drain on profitability.

Previous Discounting Experiences

Now, let me share a personal story to illustrate the importance of having a coherent pricing strategy. While most of my career has been in sales, I started out as an electrician. During that time, I was often tasked with procuring materials for specific installations we were working on. Back then, there were numerous electrical wholesalers to choose from, and the guiding principle from my supervisor was always to get the best price possible.

This usually involved spreading the order across multiple suppliers to secure the biggest discounts.

Looking back, I now see that this approach was highly ineffective. The time it took to gather all the information often outweighed the savings we achieved on individual items. However, what really puzzled me were the massive discounts that suppliers would offer. I'd call up a particular wholesaler, list out the items I needed, and hear responses like, "You get 70% off the conduit, 65% on cables, and 85% on the bulkheads." It always made me wonder - who was setting these list prices? Were they so uncoordinated with the market that they had to discount by such huge margins? And what message does that send to the customer? To me, it showed a blatant disregard for having any kind of pricing strategy that made sense.

This experience highlights the importance of having a pricing strategy that is clear, believable, and aligned with the value you offer your customers. Even though the industry has sharpened its approach in an age where price transparency is everywhere, it goes to show that clarity and consistency in pricing are crucial to how customers perceive value.

How Effective Pricing Drives Success

I genuinely believe that companies which excel in pricing strategies will deliver sustainable profitability, even in the toughest economic conditions. This makes pricing an essential, yet often underutilised, tool for driving business success. There's undoubtedly some action you can take in your business to harness this power. And to get started on that journey, let's explore how to present pricing to your sales team to ensure their tasks are as efficient and effective as possible.

Transparency is everything with your sales team when it comes to pricing. Show them exactly how a given price is derived and what it means for the profitability of your business - and their commission or bonus payouts. This approach improves their commercial knowledge and ensures they're aligned with your goals.

Over the years, I've seen a mixture of approaches from companies when it comes to pricing transparency, and my experience tells me that an open-book policy with your team is far more effective in the long run. Ultimately, your salespeople are trying to articulate value to your customers, and price is a huge part of that proposition. By being upfront with your team about how prices are set, you will empower them to make better decisions in their negotiations, creating a sense of ownership and alignment with their personal goals, and the company's objectives.

Build Efficient and Effective Processes

Efficiency and effectiveness are key to tackling core business processes, including pricing. Your sales team should have instant access to realistic list prices - prices that have been carefully considered based on customer value, competitive pressures, and operational costs, as mentioned earlier. Gone are the days of overinflated list prices that require massive discounts to seem competitive. Instead, focus on setting prices that are fair, transparent, and reflective of the value you provide.

In an ideal world, this would be the end of the discussion. You've set your list prices, they maximise profitability, your sales team sells at those prices, and your customers buy happily. But, in reality, especially in a business-to-business (B2B) setting, discounts are commonplace.

When it comes to discounts, my starting point for any commercial strategy is this: we don't need to give discounts because our list prices already meet market expectations. However, I recognise that there are times when discounts are necessary - whether to remain competitive or as a reward for something specific. Whatever your discount principles are, my advice is to always have a clear policy.

Your sales team needs to know what is expected of them, so don't complicate their day. Ensure they have clear objectives around when and how to apply discounts. Do they understand the guardrails in place? Do they know who the authorised approvers are for discount overrides? Just to say, minimising overrides is crucial, as they can drain valuable management resources.

Groove Discounting: My Pet Hate

One phenomenon that continues to irritate me is what I call "groove discounting." This occurs when sales teams habitually offer discounts that end with a 5 or 0, like 10%, 15%, 20%. When a customer pushes back on a price, the salesperson often increases the discount in these increments. It's as if they're stuck in a discounting groove, unable to break free from these standard percentages.

This practice is not only unsophisticated but also detrimental to your profitability. Imagine you're offering a 20% discount, but the customer still feels the price is too high compared to a competitor. The typical response from a salesperson is to bump the discount up to 25%, almost by reflex. But what if there was a smarter way to handle this?

Instead, I encourage your team to explore more precise discounting. For example, if 20% isn't enough, try offering 21.3% and see how the customer reacts. This incremental approach can prevent the unnecessary giveaway of margin. My gut feeling is that if you offer a price based on 21.3% and the customer is still not satisfied, they're more likely to reveal their target price, which could save you from needing to jump straight to 25%.

This approach not only protects your margins but also positions your sales team as more thoughtful and strategic negotiators, rather than order-takers who simply cave to customer demands.

A Strategic Approach to Discounts

When it comes to long-term discounts for customers, many companies base these on purchase volume or perceived competitive threats. While these approaches are common, they often lack a strategic foundation. Instead, consider a different approach: start by listing the factors that demonstrate a customer's commitment to your business and how they align with your core values. These could include timely payments, referrals, testimonials, joint marketing activities, or even that they purchase multiple services. Once you have these criteria, plot your customers on a matrix with commitment on one axis and values alignment on the other. This exercise will not only help you identify which customers truly resonate with your business but also guide you in determining who may warrant discounts.

I have provided a practical example on the next page to illustrate how this might work for you. I once consulted for a company in the service industry where pricing was a bit haphazard and so we developed this concept.

We started by identifying all the attributes that indicated a customer commitment to the business and alignment with its values. These included paying on time, providing referrals, participating in joint marketing, and being willing to give testimonials. We then plotted each customer on a four-box matrix: down the left side was their level of commitment to the business, while across the bottom was their alignment with the core values.

This clear visual representation helped us make informed decisions about pricing strategies and discounts, ultimately strengthening relationships with those customers that mattered most.

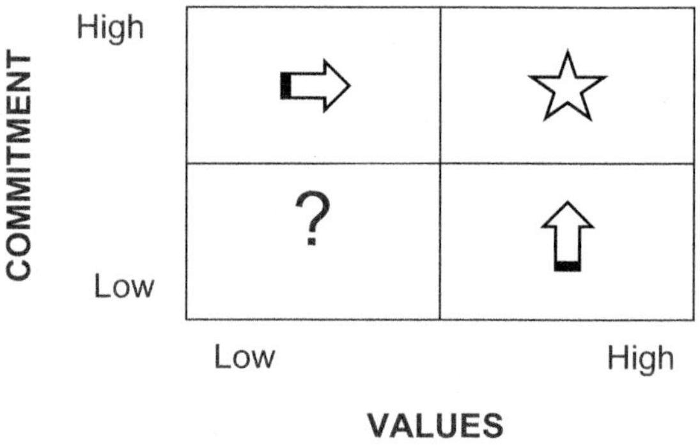

Hopefully, you can image the scenario whereby this visual representation helped us see instantly which customers were truly on board with the company. Not just in terms of revenue, but also in terms of relationship quality. It became clear that some smaller customers who didn't bring in the most revenue were actually more valuable partners due to their alignment of values and commitment. Conversely, some of the larger customers who seemed important based on scale alone were less aligned and less committed.

Evaluating and Adjusting Discounts

Once you've plotted your customers on this matrix, you can start testing and adjusting discounts. If there is a commercial benefit, reward those in the top right-hand corner who are committed and aligned with your values. For those in the bottom left, consider reassessing their discounts - perhaps they aren't as valuable to your business as you thought.

This kind of strategic approach to discounting ensures that you're not just throwing discounts around like confetti. Instead, you're rewarding true partners who are helping to grow your business in a meaningful way.

Conclusion

Pricing and discounting are critical aspects of any business, and they deserve the same strategic focus as other elements of your operation. By grasping the 1% power of pricing - where even small adjustments can lead to significant impacts - being transparent with your sales team, and applying discounts strategically, you can effectively drive profitability and customer satisfaction.

It's important to remember that your goal is to align pricing with the value you deliver. Ensure that your discounts genuinely reward the behaviours and relationships that matter most to your business. This thoughtful approach helps build loyalty among your customers.

If you can invest quality time in analysing and refining your pricing strategies, you'll be well on your way to unlocking hidden profits and building stronger, more meaningful customer relationships. With each decision you make, consider how it supports your overall vision and enhances the experience for your clients.

SALES MANAGEMENT

Lesson 6: Field Activity Levels

You'll recall the story from Lesson 4: Opportunity Pipeline, where I spoke about a former manager who once said, "When you can boast about your sales, then boast about your sales. If sales aren't so good, then boast about your order book. If the order book is empty, then you'd better rely on a strong opportunity pipeline. And if your pipeline is lacking, you'd better have a strong story about the activities you're doing to fill it." This philosophy is something that resonates deeply with me, and it underpins much of what we'll be discussing in this lesson.

This lesson jumps into the most granular aspect of that philosophy - the activity levels required to fill your pipeline. Having spent much of my career in field sales, that's where we'll focus, as I believe it's where the best business is done. However, I do acknowledge that a hybrid model has emerged, accelerated by the pandemic. While I did secure several large contracts with clients I never met in person during the pandemic, the sales cycle was noticeably longer - two to three times longer - than it would have been with face-to-face interactions. This was a real revelation for me, and it reinforced my belief that nothing quite beats getting in front of a customer.

Face-to-Face vs Digital

Rapport is crucial, and while you can build relationships through video calls and phone conversations, I believe nothing replaces those in-person moments - the walk from reception to the office, grabbing a coffee, meeting other team members, or chatting with a new employee about their experiences. You can learn a lot during these interactions, and sometimes, it's the unplanned, informal conversations that yield the most valuable insights. So, my advice to anyone in field sales is this: **get in front of your customer.**

There's something about being physically present that accelerates trust-building. Body language, eye contact, and those subtle cues that you notice in person are difficult to replicate in a digital environment. Early in my career, when I sold technical products, demonstrations were key in convincing customers to try something new. For instance, I was once selling a range of infrared thermometers for environmental health officers and quality control teams. These devices allowed for quick temperature checks of refrigerators or cold storage facilities with just a squeeze of a trigger, saving time compared to traditional temperature probes. Demonstrating this product in person increased my pipeline with numerous opportunities. People need to see, touch, and experience the value proposition firsthand.

In contrast, while digital tools have their place, they lack the tactile element that often helps solidify a deal. For example, when introducing a new piece of equipment or technology, nothing beats the impact of a live demo. You can explain the features and benefits all day long over a video call, but when you physically show the client how it works and how it will make their life easier, that's when the lightbulb moment happens. This is especially true in industries where the product's functionality is complex or where trust in the product's reliability is paramount. If a picture is worth a thousand words, then a demonstration is worth a million.

The Discipline of Field Sales

In my first big sales role, the proposition was different. The company sold hundreds of thousands of products via a distribution model, but as a Salesperson for Teesside in 2003, my role was to sell the service. My target was to make 10 face-to-face visits a day. While newer salespeople might find this daunting today, there are valuable lessons from those days that remain relevant. The discipline and structure it took to maintain that pace were instrumental in shaping my career and developing the skills that would serve me well in more complex sales environments later on.

Let's break down the numbers. My territory covered a 25-mile radius from my home in the Tees Valley, so I was never more than 30 - 40 minutes from any customer. I had around 1,800 spending accounts in my area, with an 80/20 split - 80% of revenue came from 20% of the customers. Within those accounts, multiple contacts bought from me, creating a contact base of over 5,000 people, with the same 80/20 rule applying. This meant that I needed to be strategic about how I managed my time and prioritised my efforts. With so many potential contacts, the challenge was to stay organised and focused on the activities that would deliver the highest return.

Our week was highly structured. We spent 4.5 days in the field, with Fridays reserved for admin. While this inflexibility wouldn't work for me today, it taught me the discipline needed to capitalise on the vast customer base. This structure allowed me to build momentum throughout the week, ensuring that I was always moving forward with my pipeline. This role was about physically being present, shaking hands, and building relationships.

This kind of rigidity might seem counterproductive today, especially with the abundance of digital communication tools that allow for more flexible schedules. But there's something to be said for the discipline of a well-structured week. It forces you to be intentional with your time, ensuring that you're not just busy, but productive. That discipline can easily be translated into the modern sales environment, even if the tools and methods have evolved.

A Typical Day in the Field

Let's explore a typical Tuesday. My diary looked something like this (excuse the company names):

9:00 AM: Meeting with John (Engineering Manager) at Best Steel Works in Middlesbrough.

11:00 AM: Appointment making for next Tuesday (from the car).

11:30 AM: Meeting with Bill (Facilities Manager) at Get Well Soon Hospital in Middlesbrough.

1:30 PM: Meeting with Peter (Technical Manager) at Gorgeous Foods in Stockton-on-Tees.

3:30 PM: Meeting with Alan (Senior Maintenance Engineer) at Lovely Bakery in Stockton-on-Tees.

You might notice that I only had four meetings scheduled, not ten. However, alongside each appointment, I always aimed to meet two or three additional people. When setting up a meeting, I'd ask my main contact if they could introduce me to other team members or departments. Building trust, rapport, and consistently creating value made this approach possible. This strategy was about maximising each visit, ensuring that every interaction counted. You never know who might have the next big project or who might need your services. I used Friday afternoons to plan my key contacts I wanted to call the week ahead and identify additional people who might be starting new projects or facing challenges.

Just a quick note on advanced planning. In this instance, scheduling meetings too far in advance often led to changes or cancellations, while last-minute bookings rarely worked. I found that booking appointments for 7-days ahead was the sweet spot. This balance between planning and flexibility meant I always had a full diary without overwhelming myself with too much advance planning.

Appointment Making Example

Here's how a typical appointment-making call would go (skipping the rapport-building for brevity):

"Hi Peter, last time we met, you mentioned planning for the summer shutdown around April. Since we're in the last week of May, I thought it might be a good time to discuss how we can help optimise your maintenance parts inventory. I'll be in Stockton next Tuesday afternoon and **REALLY** want to see you. Would half-past one work for you?"

"Great, it's in the diary. Actually, Peter, before I let you go, could you introduce me to your new apprentices, Mark, and Anthony? I want to ensure they're aware of the next-day service available for their maintenance items. Also, if James in Facilities is around, I'd like to catch up with him about a new range of low-energy lighting."

By the end of the call, my diary entry looked like this:

1:30 PM: Meeting with Peter (Technical Manager) at Gorgeous Foods, Stockton-on-Tees. Plus: Mark and Anthony (next-day service) and James (energy-saving lighting).

This approach allowed me to get the most out of every visit. By being proactive and asking for introductions, I was able to expand my network within each business, gaining access to more opportunities and building stronger relationships. This is a practice that has stayed with me throughout my career, and I believe it's one that every salesperson should adopt. The more people you know within an organisation, the better your chances of success. This approach allows you to build a well-connected web of relationships that support your long-term goals.

My Sales Activity Evolution

As my career evolved and I worked with more complex accounts, this level of activity wasn't always possible. Spending a full day with a client on complex problem-solving became the norm. However, the lessons from those early days stayed with me, particularly when dealing with decision-making units (DMUs) in a complex sale. There's often more than one person involved in making a final decision, and the principles of broadening your engagement within a business still stand. I've made it a habit to ask, "Who else should be at the meeting?" when setting up appointments, which has helped me build stronger relationships and gain deeper insights.

When you're dealing with complex sales, the stakes are higher, and the process is more drawn out. But the fundamentals remain the same. You need to build trust, demonstrate value, and engage with multiple stakeholders. The difference is that you have to do it on a larger scale, often over a longer period. This requires patience, persistence, and a deep understanding of your client's needs and challenges.

The sales environment is constantly evolving, but some things will never change for me. The importance of building relationships, understanding your client's needs, and being proactive in your approach will always be key to success. Whether you're making ten visits a day or spending a full day with one client, these principles will serve you well.

The Power of Discipline and Flexibility

The activity levels required to fill your pipeline are non-negotiable, whether you're working in 100% field sales or as a hybrid model. The discipline to maintain a consistent level of activity, coupled with the flexibility to adapt to each client's unique needs, is what separates successful salespeople from the rest. By getting in front of your customers, asking the right questions, and being proactive in your approach; you'll fill your sales pipeline and also build the kind of relationships that lead to long-term success.

Those early days in sales taught me the value of discipline, structure, and the importance of being present with your customers. While the sales landscape may have changed since then, these lessons remain relevant. The tools we use might be different, but the fundamentals of building relationships, understanding your client's needs, and being proactive in your approach will always be at the heart of successful sales.

The Pandemic Changed the Landscape

The pandemic has undeniably changed the way field sales operate, possibly forever. In the first week of March 2020, my schedule was packed. I had a meeting in London with an implementation partner on Monday, flew to Brussels that evening to meet with an oil company on Tuesday, stayed overnight for a meeting with a food manufacturer on Wednesday, and then flew back to London to meet a consulting group in Oxford on Thursday. By Friday, the world began to shift. I started receiving calls and emails from clients cancelling the following week's meetings due to concerns over the "virus." I'm sure you remember this too, and like many others, I didn't set foot in another client's premises until much later that year.

It took time, but eventually, we resumed visiting clients - although not with the same intensity as before. We all learned valuable lessons during those years, discovering that business can be conducted remotely. Yet, I believe most field sales professionals would agree nothing beats the energy, engagement, and fulfilment of meeting people face to face. That's what draws many of us to field sales in the first place.

We now know that today's sales environment operates in a hybrid model, blending phone calls, emails, video conferences, and in-person meetings. In my consultancy, I still aim to meet face-to-face with clients as soon as we establish a mutual understanding of their needs. My typical sales cycle begins with a 30-minute introductory call. A small number of these calls conclude there, often due to a misalignment in solutions. However, I always try to recommend alternative partners who might be able to help.

When alignment is found, I prioritise wrapping up the call quickly to schedule a much deeper discovery meeting. Depending on the client's location, this can be in person or, more often, via Microsoft Teams. The pause between the introductory call and the discovery meeting allows both parties to reflect, research, and prepare in greater detail, leading to a more valuable session. If the alignment holds, the next step is usually an on-site meeting. This is crucial to meet the team, tour their facilities, and dive deeper into their pain points. This ensures that any work undertaken is done for the right reasons and under the right conditions.

Conclusion

Everything we discussed in this lesson ties back to those early lessons we've already explored. How well is your sales team aligned with your marketing strategy? What's their value proposition? How do they engage with prospects and customers? How does lead generation impact their ability to build an opportunity pipeline? Once you answer these questions, you can define the right approach for your business.

If a video call is the most appropriate option, and it saves travel time and costs, then let them do that. However, if a field visit will provide deeper insights and strengthen relationships, then get out to the site as soon as possible. The key message here is confidence. It's all too easy for your field team to rely on the safety of their laptop to develop a pipeline. But nothing beats the rapport built from face-to-face interactions. Encourage your team to spend at least a few days a week in the field, making the most of their time. To finish, always ensure that efficiency and effectiveness drive how you manage your field sales team's activities. If you can stay committed to this approach, success will undoubtedly follow.

Lesson 7: Selling Methodology

This lesson is dedicated to how to define, select, and implement a selling methodology for your business. When I say, “selling methodology,” you might be more familiar with other terms, such as a sales process or sales cycle. In simple terms, a selling methodology refers to a structured approach or framework that guides how your sales team interacts with potential customers throughout the sales journey. It encompasses specific techniques, behaviours, and strategies designed to increase engagement, build lasting relationships, and ultimately close deals.

Different methodologies will place emphasis on various aspects of the sales process - whether it's understanding customer needs, offering tailored solutions, or prioritising long-term partnerships over short-term wins. What’s essential to remember is that it should provide a clear roadmap for your sales team to follow. This ensures consistency in how they approach each interaction, while still allowing for some level of adaptability to cater to different buyer situations and personalities.

The Allure of Sales Training

However, before we get too deep into the specifics, I’d like to offer a word of caution, drawn from my years of experience observing a common phenomenon. You’ll find that there are numerous training companies promising to transform your sales team with their own selling methodology. If you were to do a quick online search for ‘sales training,’ ‘sales process,’ or ‘sales cycle,’ you’d be flooded with options - each one claiming to have the magic formula to drive your business to unprecedented growth.

Now, don't get me wrong. I believe that many of these solutions can, in fact, be valuable to your business. However, there's an important caveat: this kind of training is only effective when viewed as part of a long-term change program. My overwhelming experience has shown me that many businesses mistakenly see sales training as a one-off event. There's often an assumption that a great sales trainer can simply walk in, energise the team, and magically elevate performance.

Typically, the business pays a substantial amount for this training. The trainer delivers a high-energy, motivational session, the team is buzzing with enthusiasm, and everyone walks away with glossy post-training materials. On the surface, it seems like the perfect recipe for success, and expectations for growth are sky-high.

Sales Training Can Be a Waste of Time

Here's something I've learned over time: I believe up to 80% of sales training ends up being a complete waste of time for most businesses. The root of the problem lies in how this training is framed. It's too often viewed as a fix-all solution that every member of the sales team must attend, regardless of their experience or actual need for it.

I'm sure you've got some seasoned salespeople in your business. Sitting through yet another sales training session is likely the last thing they need. At best, they might share some entertaining stories that the trainer can use as case studies during the workshops. At worst, they could become disruptive, challenging the principles being taught because, in their eyes, they've already "seen it all."

Embedding a Selling Methodology

The other critical issue is that, when seen as a one-off event, the training rarely becomes embedded in the day-to-day operations of the business. You may recall from our earlier lesson on the Opportunity Pipeline how I explained the importance of aligning your sales process with the customer's buying journey. In my consultancy business, I've fully embedded my sales methodology into how things operate on a daily basis. As I complete each step of the sales process, using the tools and techniques in my selling methodology, I can move seamlessly through the sales cycle.

Embedding these principles into the very fabric of your business is the key to long-term success. Below you can see a reminder of how that looks in practice for my business:

Steps	**Buying Journey**	**Sales Process**	**Pipeline Status**
1	Aware	Rapport	Initial Outreach
2	Learn	Discovery	Needs Assessed
3	Consider	Problems	Pain Known
4	Evaluate	Presentation	Solution Presented
5	Decide	Proposal	Proposal Submitted
6	Negotiate	Objections	Terms Finalised
7	Buy	Close	Won

Sales Training in Real Life

Let's explore a scenario that I've encountered many times. Picture a sales management team, energised and eager just days after their sales team has completed training on a new selling methodology from an external partner. You can imagine the scene - every opportunity, even remotely connected to the training, is analysed and scrutinised. Why? It's all about return on investment (ROI). This is often the ultimate test of any training programme. After the time and money invested, did it lead to increased revenue, saved time, or new customers?

For many businesses, investing in a brand-new selling methodology is about optimising the sales process, driving efficiency, and increasing revenue and profit. But as I mentioned earlier, this can't be viewed as a quick fix. It must be part of a long-term change programme. This involves more than just training your PEOPLE; you also need to focus on your PROCESS and SYSTEMS.

PEOPLE: **What** do we want our teams to do?

PROCESS: **How** do we want our teams to do it?

SYSTEMS: **Where** do we want our teams to do it?

Now, let's return to our scenario. Imagine you're a fly on the wall in a sales office, just a couple of days after a comprehensive sales training course designed to introduce a new selling methodology. You're observing a conversation between a sales manager and a salesperson, where the high energy of the training starts to collide with the realities of daily operations.

Sales Manager: "Hey, that sounded like a great call this morning. I overheard bits from across the office, and I was really impressed. You showed such confidence as you presented the proposal, and I could hear how well you're applying the lessons from this week's training. It's clear the new process is helping you. But I have just one question - have you sent the contract to the customer yet?"

Salesperson: "Not yet, but I'm working on it."

Sales Manager: "What? Why not? In the training, we told you that the contract should be sent immediately after the final proposal to keep everything fresh in the customer's mind. If you wait even 30 minutes, the customer's attention will shift, and you'll struggle to get them back on track."

Salesperson: "Yes, I remember. But in this instance, I can't send the contract because I haven't received sign-off from finance for the extended payment terms. We have a lot like this."

Sales Manager: "Oh, when do we usually get finance sign-off?"

Salesperson: "When Jim (Sales Director) authorises the terms in the CRM."

Sales Manager: "And when did we request this authorisation?"

Salesperson: "I did it this morning, right after presenting the final proposal to the customer."

Sales Manager: "Oh, I see. How long will it take to get Jim's authorisation and then finance's approval?"

Salesperson: "I'm not sure. I think Julie (Finance Director) is on holiday this week."

Sales Manager: "Could someone else sign it off?"

Salesperson: "Not according to what was said in last month's sales meeting."

Sales Manager: "Which meeting was that?"

Salesperson: "The one you missed. You were on holiday in Spain, remember?"

Sales Manager: "Yes, I was away. I haven't caught up on everything. What was decided?"

Salesperson: "Julie came in mid-morning and joined Jim to talk about extended payment terms. She said no contract should be sent until she's personally approved any extended terms, to avoid looking unprofessional by retracting offers later. Jim agreed and said we were giving extended terms too freely, so they want to have more control."

Sales Manager: "What do you mean by 'control'?"

Salesperson: "Jim agreed that every request for extended payment terms must be signed off by Julie, no exceptions. She wants full visibility so she can track how things evolve."

Sales Manager: "But how does that fit with the training we've just completed? It seems like there's now a big gap in the steps, and I'm not sure what that means for the overall process."

Salesperson: "Yes, I see your point. That training step doesn't seem to match the reality we're facing."

Sales Manager: "Mmmm, yes, it does seem a bit disconnected, doesn't it? I'd better have a word with Jim."

Make Training a Strategic Decision

This scenario highlights a common challenge after sales training. Even when the methodology is sound, the internal processes, approvals, and real-life conditions can create bottlenecks that undermine the intended flow. When your sales team returns from training full of enthusiasm, it's important to ensure that the new processes align with existing systems and that potential blockers, like approvals or miscommunications, are addressed in advance.

This is why embedding a sales methodology into the daily operations of your business - across all departments, not just sales - requires much more than a one-off training session. You should never simply adopt an off-the-shelf solution without first understanding how the methodology will integrate with your existing sales and business processes. If those processes are flawed or outdated to the point where you need something entirely new, that's perfectly fine. However, it's crucial to ensure that it's not just your PEOPLE being trained. You must also define what your new PROCESS will look like and determine which SYSTEMS your team will need to operate effectively.

And this often requires a more strategic approach, one that elevates the implementation above a simple, one-off training programme.

Selling Methodology Guidance

Choosing an external provider for your selling methodology is a crucial decision and ensuring that they align well with your business's existing processes and goals is perhaps the most important aspect. Here's some advice from me on how to prepare internally and what to look for in a potential partner:

Preparing Internally

Assess Your Current Sales Processes: Before you start looking for external providers, conduct a thorough review of your existing sales processes. Identify what's working well, where the gaps are, and how the new methodology needs to integrate with or improve these processes.

Define Clear Objectives: Establish clear objectives for what you hope to achieve with the brand-new selling methodology. Are you looking to improve conversion rates, shorten the sales cycle, or enhance customer relationships? Clear goals will help you evaluate potential providers more effectively.

Involve Key Stakeholders: Engage in discussions with key stakeholders from various departments - sales, marketing, finance, operations - about any new methodology. Their insights will be invaluable in identifying needs and potential constraints.

Document Current Challenges: Make a detailed list of the challenges you face with your current methodology and processes. This will help you articulate your needs to potential providers and assess whether they can address your specific issues.

Prepare Your Team: Ensure that your sales team is prepared for the upcoming changes. Communicate the potential benefits and how the new methodology will be integrated into their daily activities.

Budget and Resources: Determine your budget for the new methodology and the resources you can allocate to its implementation. This includes not just financial resources but also time and effort from your team.

Choosing the Right External Provider

Relevant Experience and Expertise: Look for providers with experience in your industry and a track record of successful implementations. They should demonstrate a deep understanding of selling methodologies and how they can be adapted to different business contexts.

Customisation Capabilities: Ensure that the provider can tailor their methodology to fit your specific business processes and challenges. Off-the-shelf solutions may not address your unique needs effectively.

Integration with Existing Systems: The provider should have the capability to integrate their methodology with your current systems and processes. This includes CRM systems, reporting tools, and other technology platforms.

Evidence of ROI: Ask for case studies or references from similar businesses that have successfully implemented their methodology. Look for tangible evidence of return on investment and improvements achieved.

Training and Support: Evaluate the level of training and ongoing support the provider offers. Effective implementation requires more than just a one-off session.

Flexibility and Adaptability: Choose a provider who demonstrates flexibility and adaptability. They should be willing to adjust their approach based on feedback and the evolving needs of your business.

Cultural Fit: The provider should align with your company's culture and values. A good cultural fit will facilitate smoother collaboration and ensure that the methodology resonates with your team.

Change Management Approach: Look for a provider with a robust change management approach. Implementing a new selling methodology often involves significant changes, and effective change management can help ensure a smooth transition.

Conclusion

My final piece of advice is this: Whatever approach you decide to take with your selling methodology, be prepared for a long-term commitment to making it work. It should never be treated as a small side project aimed at delivering quick fixes across the business. Implementing a new methodology is a significant undertaking that requires strategic insight, expert collaboration, and exceptional communication.

As previously mentioned, this must encompass more than just training your PEOPLE. You will absolutely need to refine your PROCESS and SYSTEMS as well. It's about integrating the new methodology into the very fabric of your business, ensuring that every component works together to deliver success.

Lesson 8: Key Performance Indicators

Have you ever wondered why KPIs (Key Performance Indicators) get mentioned so often in sales meetings? If you're leading a sales team, KPIs might seem like the backbone of every decision. But what exactly are KPIs in sales, why are they so important, and how can they benefit both the salesperson and their company?

Let's break it down. Sales KPIs are essentially the metrics that help track how well your sales team is performing. These can cover various aspects, from revenue growth to the number of new customers acquired, or even how many meetings a salesperson has in a week (remember my 10 meetings per day?). The beauty of KPIs is that they can be tailored to specific goals. Whether you want to track short-term sales revenue or profits or longer-term client relationships, KPIs, when implemented correctly, can offer that flexibility.

For example, if you're focusing on expanding your customer base, you might set a KPI around lead generation or conversion rates. If customer retention is your goal, your KPIs might centre around repeat business or customer satisfaction scores.

But why do we care about KPIs? What's the real benefit?

The Importance of KPIs in Sales

KPIs aren't just numbers on a spreadsheet. They should be the pulse of your sales operation. Without KPIs, you're navigating without a map - you might be moving, but you won't know if you're heading in the right direction.

KPIs provide clarity. They allow everyone on the team to see what success looks like and give measurable targets to aim for. Whether it's those all-important revenue targets, the number of sales calls, or the average deal size, KPIs set the standard for what needs to be achieved.

But it goes beyond just meeting targets. KPIs offer insight. They highlight where things are going well and, just as importantly, where improvements are needed. It's about aligning daily tasks with larger business objectives, ensuring that each salesperson's efforts contribute to the company's overarching goals.

KPIs Are Just Like Flying a Plane

I remember when I was a child, just before we left for a family holiday to Paphos in Cyprus. In those days, you were sometimes allowed to visit the cockpit of an aircraft before take-off. I felt really privileged when I was invited up front, and the sheer number of dials and instruments in front of the pilots blew me away. There were hundreds of buttons, knobs, and screens. As a young lad, it was fantastic to see, but it also made me wonder how anyone could keep track of it all. The pilot smiled and explained, "Most of these are here for specific situations, but in reality, we focus on just a few key instruments to keep the plane flying smoothly."

That experience has stayed with me over the years, and I think about it often when I reflect on sales leadership. Just like the cockpit, sales can be full of distractions. There's data everywhere, endless reports, and targets to hit. It's easy to get overwhelmed. Like flying, success in sales comes down to focusing on the important instruments - the right KPIs.

Key Sales KPIs to Consider

Here's my take on describing the key ones for sales, with a light-hearted nod to the world of aircraft – please go with it!

Revenue Growth: The Altimeter

Just as a pilot constantly checks the altimeter to know their altitude, revenue growth can be the main indicator of how well your sales team is flying. It's the ultimate measure of success. Are your efforts leading to more sales? Is the team consistently bringing in new business? Revenue growth tells you if you're climbing to new heights or slowly descending into dangerous territory. But revenue growth needs to be sustainable. A sales team that focuses too much on quick wins may gain altitude fast, but if they don't focus on long-term strategies, they risk stalling. The key is balancing new sales with customer retention and growth.

Conversions: The Heading Indicator

In aviation, the heading indicator tells a pilot whether they're flying in the right direction. For a sales team, this could be your lead conversion rate - the percentage of leads that turn into actual sales. You could have a plane full of passengers (or leads), but if you're flying in the wrong direction or focusing on the wrong leads, you'll never reach your destination. Lead conversion rate lets you know whether you're engaging with the right prospects and making the most of your pipeline. It's a great KPI for ensuring that your team is converting opportunities into revenue. If your conversion rate is low, it might be time to rethink your targeting or sales approach. On the other side, if it's high, you know your team is focused on the right targets, and their pitch is landing well.

Sales Cycle Length: The Fuel Gauge

Imagine being in a plane and not knowing how much fuel you have left. You'd be flying blind. In sales, the length of your sales cycle is like a fuel gauge. It tells you how long it takes to close deals and whether your team is being efficient with their time and resources. If your sales cycle is dragging on, you're burning fuel (or resources) without covering much ground. This can drain your team's energy, affect morale, and ultimately impact revenue. On the other hand, a short, effective sales cycle means your team is focused, streamlined, and making the best use of their time. Keeping an eye on this KPI helps you know when to refuel or when to streamline the process to make sure you're not wasting time on unnecessary steps.

Retention: The Stability Indicator

In turbulent weather, a pilot will watch the stability indicator to ensure the plane is flying smoothly. For a sales team, customer retention is that indicator. It tells you how well you're holding onto the customers you've worked so hard to acquire. Gaining new clients is fantastic but keeping them is just as important - if not more so. If your retention rates are low, it's a sign that something isn't working. Maybe your team is too focused on acquiring new customers, and they're neglecting those they already have. Or perhaps the product or service isn't meeting expectations. Either way, this KPI can alert you to issues early on so you can adjust before things get too bumpy.

Average Deal Size: The Speedometer

Finally, average deal size is your speedometer. It lets you know how quickly you're covering ground with each sale. Bigger deals usually mean you're moving faster towards your revenue goals, but focusing solely on large deals can be risky. Just like flying a plane too fast can cause turbulence, relying too much on big deals can lead to volatility if those deals don't close. Tracking average deal size helps you strike the right balance. A healthy mix of smaller, more frequent deals combined with larger, strategic wins keeps your sales pipeline full and the team moving forward at a steady pace. If the team is too focused on chasing whales, it might be time to slow down and diversify the deal sizes.

Avoiding Information Overload

Much like a pilot needs to focus on just a few instruments, sales teams should avoid being overloaded with too many KPIs. It's easy to get caught up in the noise of data, dashboards, and reports, but that can lead to paralysis or confusion. When you're staring at a hundred dials, you're more likely to miss the important ones.

As a sales leader, part of your job is to help your team filter out the distractions and focus on the KPIs that truly matter. Too many KPIs can feel like turbulence, throwing your team off course. But by zeroing in on the four or five key metrics - revenue growth, lead conversion rate, sales cycle length, customer retention, and average deal size - you're giving your team a clear path to follow.

How KPIs Can Help a Company

As a sales leader or business owner, you're responsible for making sure the team performs - and KPIs can make your life a lot easier. Imagine trying to run a business without knowing how your team is performing. You wouldn't know who's excelling, who's struggling, or where resources should be focused. KPIs provide that measurable data. You can't rely or gut feelings or assumptions – instead work on real, hard facts. You can track who's hitting their targets and who needs additional support. This level of transparency helps create a performance-driven culture.

Have you ever had a situation where half the team is working on one thing while the other half is focused elsewhere? It's chaotic. KPIs ensure that everyone is on the same page. They align individual activities with the business's broader objectives. Whether your goal is to increase market share, drive revenue, or improve customer retention, KPIs ensure the team's efforts are focused on what matters most.

One of the most significant advantages of tracking KPIs is that it helps you make smarter decisions. For example, if your KPIs show that conversion rates drop at a particular stage in the sales process, you can investigate and address the root cause. Instead of guessing, you're making data-driven decisions that can directly impact performance. Over time, this leads to optimising your entire sales process.

Not every task delivers equal value. Some actions are more profitable or impactful than others. By tracking KPIs, companies can understand which activities yield the best results and allocate their resources accordingly. If certain lead sources produce higher conversion rates, it makes sense to focus efforts and resources there. KPIs help in spotting these trends so you can adapt your approach accordingly.

How KPIs Can Help a Salesperson

For a salesperson, KPIs can feel like added pressure - another target to hit, another metric to obsess over. But when framed correctly, they can also serve as a roadmap for personal development. Each salesperson can set personal goals aligned with the team's KPIs. For example, if your team is focused on increasing lead conversion rates, individual salespeople can aim to improve their closing techniques or refine their pitching strategies.

KPIs also help to create sales team accountability. When a salesperson knows their performance is being tracked against specific metrics, they're more likely to stay focused and motivated. The knowledge that their performance is visible can encourage them - with the right level of coaching - to put in extra effort to meet or exceed their targets. This sense of accountability can lead to a stronger team dynamic, where members support one another and strive for shared goals.

On a personal level, KPIs can act as a growth tool. A salesperson can identify areas for improvement by reflecting on their performance metrics. Are they struggling to convert leads? They might invest time in training or mentoring to sharpen their skills. Are they meeting their targets but want to take it to the next level? KPIs can guide their development and help them expand their capabilities.

Conclusion

I hope the aircraft analogy helped bring the topic of KPIs to life. The reality of producing a good set of KPIs is both a science and an art. The science comes from data, metrics, and tracking performance. But the art lies in understanding how to balance those metrics to ensure your sales team remains engaged and motivated.

Remember that the journey in sales is not just about numbers; it's about people. KPIs should serve as tools for empowerment, not constraints. By selecting the right KPIs and focusing on what truly matters, you as a sales leader can create an environment where your teams can succeed. It's about aligning individual performance with your business strategy, marketing tactics, and team objectives while keeping the overall ‘destination’ in focus.

Lesson 9: Key Account Management

Looking back, I can honestly say that my time as a key account manager was one of the most rewarding phases of my career. It gave me the opportunity to build strong relationships with some of the biggest names in aerospace, defence, and large-scale manufacturing. These industries are fascinating, with all their complexities and unique challenges. But the relationships they have with key suppliers, in many ways, come down to something simple: trust. It was during this period that I truly learned what it means to become a trusted partner for my clients.

In sales, it's so easy to get caught up in the day-to-day tasks - processing orders, sorting out issues, and keeping the numbers ticking along. Don't get me wrong, all those things matter. But making a real impact? That comes down to something deeper. It was during this time that I started to understand how key account management can move beyond the transactional and into something more meaningful. That shift towards being a trusted advisor is where I found the most value.

Moving Beyond Transactions

One of the biggest shifts for me was realising that it wasn't about working with just any client, but about focusing on the right clients for a long-term partnership. Instead of being one of many suppliers, the aim was to become a partner who really understood their business and could offer something more - strategic advice, insights, and solutions that would take their business forward.

I remember a time when this approach really paid off. I was working with an aerospace client - a key account for us - and they were facing some serious supply chain issues. Their team was sourcing from a large number of suppliers, which made their system inefficient and hard to control. This wasn't just a logistical issue; it was actually holding them back from being more agile in their own operations.

Seeing this as an opportunity to *add value*, I worked closely with their procurement team. We introduced a preferred supplier solution that streamlined their process, making it much more efficient. It allowed their end-users to place orders quickly and effectively, reducing the complexity of their operations. This *value creating intervention* fundamentally improved their workflow, saved them time and money, and *improved* our position in their supply chain. We went from being *just another* supplier to becoming an integral part of their team, moving from a transactional relationship to a true partnership.

Why Key Account Management Matters

When you break it down, key account management should result in a win-win for both sides. From the customer's perspective, having a dedicated key account manager means they get someone who genuinely understands their needs and can provide tailored solutions. There's a long-term perspective in play here - a focus on solving today's issues and at the same time helping them navigate tomorrow's challenges too.

For businesses, the benefits are just as significant. Key account management helps to build stronger, deeper relationships, leading to more customer loyalty. When clients feel that you're really invested in their success, they're far less likely to look elsewhere. Even when faced with cheaper, faster, or newer alternatives; that trust makes all the difference. And we know that in business, trust equals loyalty, which ultimately results in long-term revenue.

But the real beauty of key account management lies in the insights you gain from these close relationships. By working hand in hand with your clients, you start to see trends, issues, and opportunities that others might miss. This gives you a unique edge, helping you shape the solutions you offer and also your overall business strategy. It becomes an ongoing learning process that keeps you both competitive and in tune with any market shifts.

Building Trust Takes Time

The cornerstone of successful key account management is respect. Without it, you're just another supplier, another name on a purchase order. But when clients respect you, trust your judgement, and rely on your insights, you're far more than that - you're a valuable partner. And in my experience, gaining that respect and trust takes time, consistency, and a genuine desire to help.

The industries I've worked in - whether aerospace, defence, or large-scale manufacturing – all demanded a high level of trust. There's a lot at stake and getting things wrong simply isn't an option. Building relationships in these fields requires a combination of patience, deep listening, and showing up when it matters most. It should never be about making a quick sale today. Instead, you need to be a steady, reliable presence over the long term.

I've found that when you take the time to truly understand a client's business, their goals, and their challenges, they begin to see you as more than a supplier. You become someone they can turn to for advice, support, and solutions.

And it's in these moments that you move from being just another vendor to becoming a key part of their team.

Becoming a Trusted Advisor

This idea of becoming a trusted advisor is something I've always believed in. When clients see you in this light, they don't just come to you for products or services alone. They value your insights and your ability to guide them through their most complex and tough decisions. It's a status that can only be earned through hard work, consistency, and a genuine investment in their success. Success is a word we will return to later in the book.

One example that really sticks with me is from a manufacturing client. They were struggling with a disorganised inventory system, which led to stockouts and overordering. The result was a lot of wasted time and money, and it was starting to cause operational problems. After spending time with their team, observing how they managed inventory, I suggested we introduce a managed stores solution.

This was a service we hadn't sold to them before, but we had experience with other clients. Because we'd built such a strong relationship and they trusted my insights and our experience, they were open to trying it out. We started with a small trial and the impact was immediate. Not only did it streamline their inventory management, but it also saved them significant costs.

From that point on, they viewed us as more than just a supplier - we became a partner they could rely on for valuable business insights and were happy to extend out to more sections of their inventory over the coming 8 months.

The Long-Term View

It's easy to get caught up in the chase for new clients, and while that's a critical part of growing any business, I've always believed that the real value lies in nurturing the relationships you already have. Key accounts represent enormous opportunities, but they require time and effort to develop.

For me, that means not waiting for clients to tell me what they need but anticipating it. By staying close to their business, understanding their pain points, and identifying ways we could add value before they even ask for it, I was able to position myself as an indispensable part of their team. Whether it was through finding ways to streamline their operations or simply being a consistent, reliable presence, the clients who stayed with us were the ones who felt I had their best interests at heart. That's the key - demonstrating that you're as invested in their success as they are, and that build trust.

Building trust means you are able to create a partnership that lasts. When clients trust you, they're more likely to come to you for advice, to involve you in their bigger, more complex projects, and to stay with you through the ups and downs.

In my experience, the clients who feel valued and respected are the ones who are open to exploring new opportunities with you. And from a business perspective, these relationships are the ones that drive long-term growth. The trust you build allows for deeper engagement and greater insight into what clients really need, helping you evolve and grow alongside them.

Strategies for Account Management

If you're looking to take your key account management strategy to the next level, here are a few immediate changes you can make that I've found will work well:

Maintain Regular Contact: It's important to stay in touch with clients beyond just the moments when a deal is on the table. Proactively checking in helps you understand their current challenges and offer support where you can. Regular communication builds trust and shows that you genuinely care about their success.

Create Value: Clients deeply appreciate when you take the time to understand their unique needs and provide tailored solutions. Generic solutions can feel impersonal and less effective, especially when building long-term partnerships. By offering specific insights or resources that directly benefit their business, you strengthen the relationship and demonstrate your commitment to their success.

Be Proactive: Instead of waiting for clients to come to you with problems, keep an eye out for opportunities to help improve their business. This could involve suggesting improvements, sharing industry trends, or identifying potential challenges they may not have recognised yet. Being proactive not only adds value but also positions you as a trusted advisor.

Listen Very Carefully: Feedback from clients is incredibly valuable for your growth and their satisfaction. Regularly check in to ensure they're happy with your services and that you're addressing their evolving needs. Listening attentively allows you to make adjustments and demonstrates that you value their input.

Commit to Success: Show your clients that you are truly dedicated to continuously improving the services and solutions you offer. This could be through innovative approaches, regular performance reviews, or simply being available when they need support. Your commitment to their success encourages long-term loyalty.

If you focus on these areas, I believe you'll strengthen your key accounts and also build deeper, more meaningful relationships that will drive long-term success for both you and your clients.

Conclusion

The lessons I've learned as a key account manager show that key account management is about far more than just handling large volumes of transactions from your biggest customers. It's your best opportunity to build lasting connections that drive long-term growth for both you and your clients.

Reflecting on my experiences, I've come to understand that the real value of key account management lies in how it transforms business relationships. This perspective has shaped my career and continues to guide the way I approach my consulting work and sales strategy. If you can move beyond simply managing day-to-day transactions and instead focus on nurturing meaningful relationships, key account management will become a cornerstone of your business.

Lesson 10: Account Segmentation

Account segmentation has been like an unshakable weight on my back throughout my career. If you've ever worked in the corporate space, you'll be all too familiar with the annual reshuffling of territories, account alignments, and my personal favourite – the classic move from global to regional (and then sometimes back again, just for fun). It's one of those tasks that sounds strategic and forward-thinking, but let's face it, it often ends up feeling like someone's thrown your meticulously planned work into a blender.

For most salespeople, it's one of the most demotivating times of the year, especially when the reshuffling doesn't work in their favour. Imagine this: You've spent two solid years building a key account from the ground up. You've mapped out the decision-makers, know the client's strategy inside and out, and even have a long-term growth plan in place. Things are finally about to take off – you've become their trusted advisor, and success is within reach. But then, the dreaded news hits: "We're making some strategic changes to our account structures." Translation? Boundary shifts. Territory changes. And now, you have to hand off your golden account to someone new, just as it's about to flourish. That's a heart-stopping moment for any salesperson, and it can feel like the rug's been pulled from under you.

Over the years, I've seen more account segmentation strategies come and go than I care to count. Some of them have changed as quickly as new leadership arrives. One minute, the mantra is "regional ownership is king" – the idea being that those local leaders, who often have P&L responsibility, should make all the decisions on how best to manage accounts in their region. It makes sense on paper. After all, these regional managers are responsible for their budgets, and it stands to reason they'd want control over the resources allocated to their accounts. Fair enough, right?

Then, a few years later, a new leader comes along with a new perspective. "We're not fully leveraging the potential of our global accounts," they say. "We need to group all of our energy accounts across the world under one global team to streamline our approach." Sounds like a grand idea, doesn't it? Suddenly, all the energy sector accounts are reallocated to the newly formed Energy Sector Team. The team is excited, they present their shiny new strategy at the annual conference, and off they go, ready to conquer the world.

But predictably, it doesn't take long before cracks start to show. Fast forward a year, and two country managers begin complaining. Their regional energy accounts, which inconveniently are still tied to their local targets, aren't being managed as well as they should be. Why? Because Terry, the new global account manager who's based in Ireland, isn't particularly fond of hopping on flights to Brazil or Mexico every other week. As tensions build, reports are generated, and soon, the same bright minds who dreamt up the global segmentation plan are now muttering, "You know what? Maybe we should hand these accounts back to regional ownership to ensure they get the attention they deserve."

And so, the cycle repeats.

It's a scenario I've seen play out time and time again. So, what's the lesson here? How do you stop this merry-go-round of account segmentation from disrupting your business, demotivating your sales team, and let's not forget, confusing the life out of your customers?

The key takeaway, if nothing else, is consistency. Consistency in account management, in ownership, and in the strategy that underpins it all. Look, I'm a huge fan of continuous improvement – I fully recognise that businesses need to evolve and adapt. However, too much change, especially when it comes to account ownership, can be incredibly disruptive. As much as possible, avoid swapping account managers too frequently. Think about the long-term relationship your sales team builds with their accounts. Handing an account from one manager to another every year not only demotivates your team but also risks damaging the trust and rapport they've worked so hard to establish with the client.

So, as you read on, I hope you find some practical insights on how to build a segmentation strategy that works for your business – one that balances the need for strategic growth with the need for consistency.

Account Segmentation Strategies

If you've been in sales, you've likely encountered every variation under the sun, from regional models to sector-specific approaches. While each strategy has its merits, the challenge is figuring out what works best for your business. After all, no two businesses are the same, and what works for one business doesn't necessarily work for another. But before we dive into specifics, let's take a step back and look at why account segmentation is such an essential part of a sales strategy.

At its core, segmentation is all about prioritisation. You can't treat every account equally – some customers represent far greater potential than others. The challenge is determining how to break up your customer base in a way that enables your sales team to focus on the most valuable opportunities while ensuring no one falls through the cracks. Now, onto the different approaches you might consider:

Geographic Segmentation

This is the classic approach – splitting your accounts based on regions or territories. It's simple, straightforward, and ensures that customers in each area have a dedicated sales team or individual who understands the local market dynamics. Geographic segmentation is often the first choice for businesses with widespread customer bases, particularly those that span multiple countries.

The advantage? Local focus. Sales teams in each region are likely to be more in tune with the cultural, economic, and legal nuances that can impact their accounts. If you're operating across different markets with varying challenges, a localised approach can be effective. It allows your team to get close to their accounts, build deeper relationships, and be physically present when needed.

The downside, however, is that it doesn't always align with how your customers operate. In a globalised world, many of your key accounts probably work across multiple regions. Having a different salesperson for each country can lead to fragmented communication and inconsistent service. This can frustrate customers who expect a cohesive experience no matter where they're located.

Industry or Vertical Segmentation

This approach groups accounts based on their industry or the verticals they serve. If your business operates in multiple sectors – say, manufacturing, healthcare, and finance – industry segmentation allows you to build sales teams that specialise in those areas. These teams become experts in the unique challenges and opportunities of each industry, making them far better equipped to provide relevant solutions to their customers.

The key benefit here is expertise. By focusing on a specific industry, your salespeople can speak the same language as their customers. They'll understand the industry's regulations, trends, and pain points, which makes them much more valuable to their clients. If you're selling into highly technical sectors, this kind of expertise can be a real differentiator.

However, this model isn't without its challenges. The major one being that industries are rarely confined to one geographic location. Take the energy sector, for instance. You might have major energy clients in Europe, Asia, and the Americas, and they may prefer to have a single point of contact who can address their needs across all markets. If your sales teams are siloed by industry but operate only locally, you risk creating confusion and complexity for your global clients.

Revenue-Based Segmentation

Another approach to account segmentation is to group your clients based on their size or revenue potential. This model often breaks down into categories like small, medium, and large accounts, or even key versus standard accounts. Larger, more profitable accounts might be given to more experienced salespeople, while smaller accounts are managed by junior salespeople or inside sales teams.

The appeal here is obvious – focus your best resources on

the accounts with the greatest potential. Your star salespeople can spend their time nurturing relationships with large clients, creating bespoke solutions, and ensuring these accounts grow over time. Meanwhile, smaller accounts still get attention, but perhaps from a junior team member or through automated processes.

However, revenue-based segmentation can sometimes lead to neglecting smaller accounts that have the potential to grow into big ones. Just because a customer isn't generating huge revenue now doesn't mean they won't be a significant player in the future. If your strategy is purely focused on the 'here and now,' you may miss nurturing future opportunities.

Global vs. Regional Segmentation

This is where things start to get a bit more complex, particularly for businesses operating on a global scale. Do you create a global account management team to handle multinational clients, or do you let regional teams manage accounts based on where they're headquartered?

The global model centralises decision-making and ensures consistent service across borders. It's great for clients who expect a unified approach, particularly those who operate across multiple regions. Global account managers can coordinate activities across countries, ensuring there's no duplication of effort or miscommunication.

On the other hand, regional segmentation allows for greater focus and attention at the local level. Customers who value a close, hands-on relationship may prefer to have a dedicated salesperson in their region. It also enables your team to respond quickly to local challenges, something that can be difficult when account managers are halfway across the world.

Finding a balance between these two models is often the hardest part of global account management. Some businesses opt for a hybrid approach, where global accounts are managed by a central team but with support from local salespeople who can handle the day-to-day interactions.

Product-Based Segmentation

In this model, you segment accounts based on the products or services they purchase. This works particularly well for companies with diverse product lines, as it enables your sales team to specialise in the specific products they sell. For instance, if your business offers both software and hardware solutions, you could have separate sales teams for each, ensuring they develop deep product knowledge and can better serve their customers.

The downside here is the potential for overlap. Customers who buy across multiple product categories might get frustrated if they have to deal with different salespeople for each one. If communication isn't streamlined, there's also a risk that important information falls through the cracks.

Getting Started

Starting your account segmentation strategy might feel a bit overwhelming, but if you take the time to think things through before diving in, you'll see greater success. This initial groundwork will certainly help you maximise your future sales potential and enhance customer relationships. Analysing your existing customer data and identifying key characteristics will help you create meaningful segments.

Define Your Objectives: Start by clarifying the goals you want to achieve through segmentation. Are you looking to enhance customer satisfaction, increase sales, or improve how you allocate resources? Having clear objectives will guide your segmentation efforts and help you measure their effectiveness over time.

Gather Data: Collect relevant data about your current customer base to gain insights into their behaviour and preferences. This could include demographics, purchase history, account size, industry, and geographical location. Using your CRM system or customer databases can help ensure you have a comprehensive view of your accounts, allowing you to make informed decisions.

Choose Your Segmentation Criteria: Decide on the criteria you'll use to segment your accounts. Common approaches include geographic location, industry, account size, or product usage. Focus on criteria that align with your objectives and allow for meaningful differentiation among accounts. This will enable you to tailor your strategies more effectively.

Create Segments: Once you've selected your criteria, group your accounts accordingly. Aim for segments that are significant enough to make an impact but distinct enough to justify tailored strategies. This might involve creating categories such as key accounts, growth accounts, and standard accounts, each of which will require different approaches.

Develop Tailored Strategies: For each segment, design customised strategies that address their unique needs and characteristics. This could include specific sales approaches, targeted marketing messages, or dedicated customer service initiatives.

Monitor and Adjust: Regularly review the effectiveness of your segmentation strategy. Gather feedback from your sales team and clients to understand what's working and what isn't. Be open to adjusting, as necessary. The goal is to create a dynamic strategy that evolves alongside your business and customer needs.

Conclusion

When developing your own account segmentation strategy, think about sustainability. Yes, refine and improve over time, but don't lose sight of the importance of stability for both your team and your customers. Segmentation should be designed to empower your salespeople to develop deeper relationships with their accounts, not to leave them wondering if they'll still have the same portfolio next year.

And remember, when those inevitable strategic changes do come, handle them with care. Understand the impact on your team and make sure you communicate the 'why' behind the change. That little bit of transparency can go a long way in softening the blow when someone has to hand over an account they've spent years nurturing. Because, trust me, the last thing you want is your top salesperson giving you that "not this again" look as they prepare to say goodbye to yet another hard-earned client.

SALES DEVELOPMENT

Lesson 11: Recruitment and Retention

Before we get into this lesson, I want to clarify that I'm not a professional recruiter or HR advisor. If you have specific challenges related to recruitment or retention, seeking specialist advice would be highly beneficial. My goal in this section is to share my experiences - both successes and setbacks - in sales recruitment and retention for your reflection in your own business.

Interestingly, my first attempt to land an industrial sales role after transitioning from maintenance engineering hit a roadblock early on. Despite spending almost a decade using the very products I aspired to sell, the feedback from potential employers was always the same: "You don't have any sales experience."

I wasn't one to fade into the background, especially when I had my mind set on something. Building a career in industrial sales was my goal, and I was determined to find a way to gain the sales experience needed to complement my technical skills. But how could I do that and stand a chance against other candidates who already had that experience?

It turns out my love for cars offered the solution. Like many lads in their teens, I was always buying and selling cars in the hope of one day owning my dream Ford Fiesta XR2i. So, the decision to pursue a role as a car salesperson seemed like a natural next step. Although my parents were probably a little sceptical, I knew I had to give it a go.

However, there was still one issue: I had no formal sales experience. I was worried that car dealerships might turn me away for the same reasons industrial sales roles had. Knowing my CV alone wasn't going to stand out, I decided to take a different approach - something a bit bolder that would get me noticed.

This was back in the days when the Yellow Pages was still in use. Armed with it, I noted down the addresses of every main car dealership in the area: Ford, Vauxhall, Renault, Audi, BMW, Citroën, Toyota, and more. In total, I had a target list of 18 dealerships. I printed 18 copies of my CV, took a day off work, put on my best shirt and tie, and set off to visit them one by one.

At each dealership, I walked up to the receptionist and confidently said, "Hi, I'm Paul. I'd love to quickly meet the Franchise Manager to discuss any potential sales roles." To my surprise, most receptionists were happy to help, and before I knew it, I was being introduced to the Franchise Managers (or New Car Sales Managers, as they are also known).

The meetings varied. Some were quick handshakes followed by a polite passing of my CV, while others led to more promising conversations, with follow-up dates set for future discussions. But the standout moment came at a Renault dealership.

The Franchise Manager greeted me, asked what I was after, and then, to my amazement, immediately invited me to sit down for a coffee. We chatted for a good 45 minutes, and by the end of our conversation, he offered me a position as a New Car Sales Executive on the spot. My bold move had paid off, and he saw something in me that was different from those who had gone through the conventional process.

That role was a turning point for me. I had a fantastic time at the dealership, learning the ins and outs of sales. It gave me the foundation I needed to eventually secure my dream role in industrial sales. Since then, my recruitment journey has been more traditional, but I've always tried to bring something unique to the interview process - something unexpected. And I'd say it's worked out well.

My Advice for Recruitment

One of the biggest lessons I've learned about recruitment and retention in sales is that personality will always trump skills. My experience at Renault taught me that. I demonstrated my ability to convince someone to buy into me first, which meant we built rapport - and building rapport is really the first step in any sales cycle.

Over the years, I've worked for some large PLCs, and while formal HR policies and procedures must be followed, I've found that integrating some social interaction into the recruitment process makes all the difference. My top tip? Create an opportunity for some social time with potential candidates. When I've recruited, I always make sure to organise a social event before finalising a decision.

It doesn't have to be elaborate. It could be as simple as meeting for coffee with a few members of the team they'd be working with. Sometimes, it's a meal at a local restaurant where they can feel comfortable in familiar surroundings. For senior positions, it might even be a dinner with executives. The specifics of the event don't matter as much as the intent behind it. Taking the time to step away from the formalities of the selection process allows you to truly get to know the person beyond their CV.

This approach not only helps you select the right candidate, but it also positively impacts your retention. Candidates feel a stronger connection to both you and the company when they see that you've made an effort to learn about them as individuals. It's this personal connection that often encourages people to stay longer in their roles.

Even when I've been on the other side of the table, being recruited, if a social event wasn't offered, I would often request one. I've had a variety of experiences: spending a full day on the road with an existing salesperson to get a feel for the day-to-day operations and see how they rated the company; a half-day in the office with the team I'd be leading to gauge what I'd be taking on and how I'd need to respond; and even a flight to Frankfurt to meet my future boss's boss, to understand their expectations for success. I've also had more informal meetups, like grabbing coffee and a pastry at Starbucks with peers in the role or joining in on beer and curry nights (my favourite).

I believe that taking these extra steps can significantly enhance the recruitment experience, both for you as the hiring manager and for the candidate. Early rapport-building plays a vital role, not only in their induction and onboarding (which I'll explore in the next lesson), but also in their long-term commitment to the company.

Hire Slowly for The Best Outcomes

When you're in a sales leadership position, it can often feel like a race to fill a vacancy. In that rush, I've seen mistakes happen - especially with candidates who seem impressive in the interview but don't hold up under further scrutiny. That's why it's important to have a solid recruitment process when hiring for salespeople or sales managers.

Below are the key steps I follow in my process. As always, your HR team should guide you on the right course of action for your business, but I hope these suggestions are helpful.

Step 1: Start with an initial interview to review their background, the talent they can bring, the growth opportunities you can offer, and to establish some early rapport. This sets the tone for a more in-depth assessment later.

Step 2: Next, conduct a competency-based interview with carefully selected questions. These questions should evaluate how well the candidate is likely to perform in the role, and it allows you to create a clear benchmark for comparing candidates, especially if you have multiple people at this stage. At this point, I also ask candidates to give a presentation on a relevant subject. Send the brief at least a week before the interview to give them ample time to prepare. This step is crucial as it allows you to see how well they interact with different people in the room and how effectively they handle questions.

Step 3: Hold a social event, as mentioned earlier. By this stage, you're likely down to your final one or two candidates, so taking time to get to know them in a more informal setting is invaluable. If time is tight for the candidate, you can combine this with the previous step or roll it into the next one.

Step 4: Always have someone who hasn't been involved in the process interview the candidate for a final time. This fresh perspective is important. Brief this person on what you like about the candidate, where you think they'd add the most value, and any areas where they might need to develop. This will allow your final interviewer to explore new angles and ensure that not only is the candidate the right fit for the company, but that your company is the right fit for them.

Always Be Respectful of Time

My last point on this topic is to always respect the candidate's time. I've seen countless posts on LinkedIn where people share their frustrations over long, complex, drawn-out recruitment processes, only to receive a generic email saying, "thanks, but no thanks." You've got to put yourself in the candidate's shoes. More often than not, they already have a job, meaning they've had to take time off work to come and visit you. While they'll understand that you have a process to follow, you should always be flexible and considerate of their circumstances.

For instance, I've conducted interviews after 5pm to accommodate someone's schedule, and I've also travelled to meet candidates when coming to the office wasn't feasible for them. If you want the right people, you have to do the right thing.

Managing Sales Retention

There are many facets that can help you develop a strong sales retention strategy. In our lessons within the Business Development section, we explored how creating alignment between sales and marketing can enhance performance, how a well-developed value proposition can streamline customer messaging, how a solid lead generation strategy helps you continually fill and execute on your opportunity pipeline, and of course, how pricing well ensures success.

In the Sales Management section, we discussed how maintaining optimal levels of customer activity can prove valuable, the importance of investing in a clear and robust sales methodology for all customers (especially key accounts), how to align territories for efficiency and effectiveness, and the necessity of clear, simple-to-understand performance measures.

Even in this Sales Development section, we'll cover induction and onboarding, the importance of targeted training for your team's success, and how coaching for high performance plays a key role. All of this can significantly impact your retention levels. If your team believes in your strategies, sees results, and feels like they can succeed, they're more likely to stay.

However, retention begins far earlier than any of this, and that's why I mention it in this section. I believe that retention starts from the very first interaction a candidate has with your company. What kind of experience do they have? Do they feel this is a company where they can build a lasting career? Have you provided them with an opportunity to assess you as a potential employer, rather than it being a one-sided evaluation?

Conclusion

I have a straightforward message to convey: from the very first meeting, always ask yourself, "What do we need to do as an organisation to help this person start their career with us on the right foot?" Getting it right from the beginning increases the chances of a successful journey throughout their time with you.

Lesson 12: Induction and Onboarding

Sitting down to write this chapter feels fitting because I recently caught up with an old sales manager from years ago. During our meeting, we found ourselves reflecting on a word that's become quite common today: 'onboarding.' Ten years ago, it wasn't really a term we used. It's one of those that's made its way over here from the US. Back then, we simply called it 'induction.' But as we reminisced about those early days, we realised that what we experienced wasn't just induction; it was a true onboarding process, even if we didn't have the language for it back then.

To me, induction and onboarding are similar but distinct. Induction is that initial stage – the first couple of days where the aim is to help a new person settle in. You get the introductions done, show them around, and sort out the basics: IT systems, health and safety, company policies. It's about making someone feel welcome and getting them ready to start.

Onboarding, though, is a much broader and longer process. It goes beyond the surface, covering weeks or even months. This is where you dig into the specifics of their role, offer training, set clear goals, and really embed them into the company culture. It's about integrating them into the business fully, ensuring they build strong relationships with key people and are set up for long-term success.

When I started my first big sales role, I had no idea I was about to embark on such a thorough process. Yes, I knew it was going to be intense based on the plan I'd been given, and the hotel block booking near the HQ was a sign that I'd be away for a while. But the entire induction and onboarding programme lasted three months – far beyond what I had expected.

The first days were just like I described earlier. It was all about settling in, meeting people, getting my laptop and phone set up, and finding out which pool car I'd be using (a green VW Passat Estate, for the record!). We were given a top-level overview of the company's vision, strategy, and priorities. That was the induction part – getting acquainted with the essentials.

But then, the real onboarding kicked in. I was part of a group of six recent sales starters, and we were soon diving deep into the company's sales strategies, learning every process we'd ever need, and becoming familiar with the tools and systems that would become our everyday lifelines. Those first few weeks were intense, to say the least – I don't think I saw daylight much during that period – but by the end, I felt ready to make an impact.

And that was just the beginning. The onboarding wasn't over – not by a long shot. We moved into month two, and instead of being left to fend for myself, I had a mentor who took me out on joint customer visits. We weren't just out for a chat either – this was about embedding the lessons I'd learned back at HQ. My mentor joined me on my visits, offering guidance and feedback that helped me develop my skills further. Towards the end of month two, I was back at the HQ, adding another layer to my ever-increasing knowledge. Everything started to click into place, and I genuinely felt like part of the team.

By month three, I was flying solo, out on the road seeing customers. But I still wasn't alone. I had the full support of a brilliant HQ team, just a phone call away, and a mentor who could be with me in 40 minutes if needed. That safety net gave me the confidence to build my territory, knowing I had backup if I hit any bumps in the road.

Of course, my manager was working closely with me throughout those first three months, but it was the combination of training, mentoring, and ongoing support that made the biggest impact. Even when I was signed off from my probation after six months, I wouldn't say the onboarding process ended. It felt like it continued throughout my entire career there. As I moved into more senior roles, there was always a sense of being onboarded into each new position, helping me to establish myself and succeed.

Looking back, it's clear that the time and effort invested in that process weren't just about ticking boxes or completing training modules. It was about deeply embedding new people into the fabric of the company. And for me, that's what real onboarding is all about – setting people up for success, for the long haul.

Since moving on from my time there, I've consistently applied the lessons I learned in every company and sales team I've led. There's always been a deep sense of satisfaction in watching new people grow in their roles over time. I believe it's because of the investment we make in those crucial early days, weeks, and months.

We didn't just introduce new people and leave them to figure things out – we embedded them into the company, and that made all the difference. In my experience, when you take the time to build a solid foundation for people at the start, the long-term rewards follow. They become more confident, more competent, and ultimately more successful. And as a sales leader, there's nothing more rewarding than seeing someone grow and flourish, knowing that the effort you put into them from day one has made a lasting impact.

Creating Program

What would a world-class induction and onboarding programme do for your business? Can you envision what it looks like, sounds like, and feels like? Whatever you have in mind, it should always be founded on establishing a solid platform for new team members, ensuring they are set up for long-term success, and helping them genuinely feel like part of the team from day one.

Drawing from my experiences, I've seen how a thoughtfully designed onboarding programme can significantly impact a new starter. With that in mind, I'd like to share a basic structure for how you may approach creating a bespoke programme tailored to your organisation.

Pre-Arrival Preparation

Welcome Communications: Before the new person even arrives, it's important to make them feel welcomed and valued. This can be as simple as sending a welcome email with a friendly note about what to expect, a rundown of their first day, and perhaps a few introductions to their new team. Getting them excited and informed before they start makes a significant difference.

IT and Workspace Setup: Nothing says 'we're prepared for you' like having their workspace and IT equipment ready to go. Ensuring that their computer, email accounts, and any other necessary tech are set up before their first day helps them hit the ground running. It's these little touches that help reduce first-day jitters and allow them to focus on integrating into the team.

Effective Induction

Orientation Program: The induction phase kicks off with an orientation that covers the basics – perhaps a tour of the office, introductions to key team members, and an overview of company policies. It's all about making them feel at home and ready to start. A friendly, engaging orientation can set a positive tone for their entire experience with you.

Role-Specific Training: Once the basics are covered, it's time to start any role-specific training. This is where you give them the specifics on their job description, key objectives, and initial tasks. Practical training sessions where they get hands-on with the tools and systems they'll use in their role are invaluable. It's about equipping them with everything they need to get started confidently.

Comprehensive Onboarding

Long-Term Integration: As I have previously discussed, onboarding isn't just about the first few days – it's a longer-term process designed to help new people fully integrate into their role and the company. This means structured training that goes beyond the basics, covering more advanced aspects of their job and company culture.

Goal Setting and Personal Development Plans: Having clear, achievable goals are essential. They will help new people understand what's expected and how they can succeed. Creating development plans that outline short-term objectives and long-term growth opportunities keeps them motivated and focused. Regular check-ins with managers or mentors also help track their progress and address any issues that might come up.

Cultural Immersion: Integrating into the company culture is just as important as learning the job specifics. This can be achieved through team-building activities, informal meetups, and participation in company events. Helping those new people understand and adapt to the company culture ensures they feel like a true part of the team.

Ongoing Support and Mentorship

Assigning a Mentor: A mentor can be a lifeline. They provide ongoing support and guidance, helping your new people navigate their role and the company environment. Regular meetings with a mentor also offers a chance to discuss progress, seek advice, and tackle any challenges head-on.

Continuous Feedback: Feedback is key to your personal development. Implementing a system for regular feedback – both from peers and managers – helps your new people understand their performance and areas for improvement. Balancing constructive challenge with positive reinforcement also helps to them build confidence and keeps them motivated.

Training and Development Opportunities: Continuous learning opportunities keep new people engaged and help them develop their skills further. Offering additional training sessions, workshops, or access to industry resources shows that you're invested in their growth.

Evaluating and Enhancing the Process

Gathering Feedback: To keep the process effective, gather feedback from new people. Surveys, interviews, and feedback forms provide valuable insights into their experience and highlight areas for improvement.

Reviewing and Updating: Regular reviews of the process help ensure it stays relevant and effective. Incorporate feedback and adapt to changes in the company or industry to keep the process up to date. Focus on continuous improvement to meet new challenges and expectations.

Measuring Success: Track key metrics like time to proficiency, employee retention rates, and job satisfaction to measure the success of your onboarding process. Analysing these metrics gives you a clear picture of how well the process is working and where adjustments might be needed.

Conclusion

I urge you to invest in your new team members from day one and to embrace a continuous onboarding approach. The reason onboarding should never be seen as a one-time event is that your business is always evolving. As your organisation adapts and grows, your people need to evolve alongside it. By adopting a culture of ongoing development, you ensure that your team remains engaged, skilled, and aligned with your company's goals.

Lesson 13: Mentoring and Coaching

Let's address the elephant in the room, one that always seems to come up whenever I talk about mentoring and coaching. You've probably asked yourself the same question, haven't you? "What's the difference between mentoring and coaching?"

I've often thought about how people tend to blur the lines between mentoring and coaching, even though they're distinct approaches. Let me share how I see it.

Mentoring is typically a longer-term relationship where someone with more experience helps guide and support the growth of another person. Think of it as passing on wisdom. The main objectives are sharing personal insights, lessons learned over the years, and helping someone navigate their career path or personal development. When I mentor, I'm drawing on my own experiences to offer guidance, a bit like shining a light on the path ahead.

Coaching, on the other hand, is more focused on helping someone unlock their own potential. It's not so much about sharing my own experiences, but rather asking the right questions to help someone find their own answers. Coaching tends to be more structured and goal-oriented, aiming to improve specific skills or overcome challenges. It empowers someone to reach their next level, without necessarily being prescriptive about how to get there.

Both mentoring and coaching have their place, and I've used both approaches throughout my career. The key is knowing when to offer advice as a mentor, and when to step back and let someone figure it out with the right support as a coach. It's that balance that can really make a difference.

When I reflect on my career, I can't help but think about the mentors who played a pivotal role in shaping the path I've walked. Mentorship has been a powerful influence for me, and I believe that sharing a few of these experiences might shed some light on how it can truly make a difference in someone's journey.

My Memorable Mentors

My first official mentor had been at the company a full ten years before I joined, so he was well-placed to guide me. It's worth noting that he's still with the company today, which speaks volumes about both him and that company as a great place to work.

All new starters in sales were assigned a mentor, typically from an adjoining territory. On certain days, we could be within a stone's throw of each other, only split by postcode boundaries. It felt reassuring to know he wasn't far away, both geographically and professionally.

When you first start a new role, everything can feel overwhelming. With a business as vast as this one, navigating your way to the right people and processes could be challenging. But with his 10 years of experience ahead of me, there wasn't a single question I asked that he couldn't answer. And that's where he truly shone as a mentor - whenever I needed help, he was always there with a solution.

What made him special in those early days was his unwavering support. He didn't challenge me or question my approach; he didn't ask what I thought or push me in a different direction. He was simply there whenever I needed him, offering practical answers and guidance. And at that point in my career, that's exactly what I needed - a steady, knowledgeable presence to lean on.

On a personal level, I have another mentor. We've been good friends since 2012, having met through a social group. There's a bit of an age gap between us, with me being slightly more experienced career-wise. When we first met, I was already working my way up the ladder, with a few success stories - and battle scars - to show for it. He, on the other hand, was just starting out on his career journey, so my support and guidance came in handy when he faced strategic decisions, process puzzles, or people challenges.

Much like how my first mentor had been there for me, I was there for my friend whenever he needed advice, a sounding board, or someone who could offer an opinion based on real-world experience. He didn't need a coach for the type of problems he was facing - his managers covered that - but he did need someone to show him a way forward. He would take the idea, put his own unique spin on it, and bring it to life in a way that reflected his flair and personality, which I always admired.

Interestingly, after achieving enormous success in the corporate world, he went on to start his own business, about five years before I launched mine. Then, the tables turned - he became my mentor as I was getting my consultancy off the ground. It's been fantastic being able to lean on him in the same way he once leaned on me. Now, with both of us being a bit older and wiser (and both coaches), our dynamic has evolved as my business became established. Rather than the old "I ask, you tell" style, we work through business challenges together, using proven coaching techniques like thoughtful questioning, deep listening, and holding each other accountable.

My Coaching Experiences

I was first introduced to coaching in my late twenties. There was a brilliant initiative across the business aimed at helping managers develop their coaching skills to improve team performance in all areas. Coaching can sometimes be dismissed as a bit "fluffy," but I saw firsthand how coaching could really transform under performance into high achievement. The skills I picked up during that time were instrumental in getting the best from my team.

Amongst my leadership peers, we had a simple motto: *stop telling and start asking*. Those words, as simple as they are, can be the beginning of something truly impactful. If you're thinking about how to improve your own coaching style, start right there - *stop telling and start asking.*

During my time at another business, I was fortunate to be selected for a one-year senior leadership development programme. As part of that, I was assigned my own coach. She was from an external company and ran her own coaching business. The adjustments I made through her coaching were truly life changing. At that point, I felt like I needed to redefine my purpose. I had achieved many of my goals, both personally and professionally, but felt in a rut.

She helped me find new passions through some challenging sessions, and that process reignited my career in ways I hadn't experienced before. The challenges she set helped me understand what high-end, one-on-one coaching is all about. I've since taken some of the techniques I learned from her and applied them when working with my own team.

Introduction to Formalised Coaching

When I was working with my personal coach, I often wondered whether I should formalise my coaching by becoming accredited. Life, as it often does, got in the way, and I didn't get around to it until 2024 - six years after my time with her. By then, I'd been practising coaching in the workplace almost every day and felt like I was about a 6 out of 10 compared to what I believed a great coach could deliver. I was also fascinated by NLP - not Natural Language Processing, but Neuro-linguistic Programming.

Put simply, NLP is a psychological approach that explores the connection between neurological processes (neuro), language (linguistic), and behavioural patterns (programming) learned through experience. The idea is that these elements interact to shape how we perceive the world, communicate with others, and respond to situations. NLP aims to help people change their thoughts and behaviours to achieve specific outcomes or goals.

Here's how it breaks down:

Neuro: This is all about the nervous system and how we take in information through what we see, hear, feel, and so on. Essentially, it's how we build our perception of the world around us.

Linguistic: Language plays a key role in shaping how we think and act. The words we use, both in our heads and in conversations, can influence our emotions, beliefs, and ultimately, our actions.

Programming: Over time, we develop patterns - think habits or automatic responses. NLP helps us 'reprogram' these so we can react differently, especially when we're trying to overcome challenges or aim for better outcomes.

NLP is widely used in coaching, personal development, and business, and it can also be incredibly beneficial in therapy. At its heart, it's a valuable tool for improving communication, increasing confidence, managing emotions, and helping us move past those limiting beliefs that often hold us back. By addressing these unproductive behaviours, NLP opens up opportunities for more positive and effective ways of working and living.

While I wanted to achieve a formal coaching accreditation, I also recognised the immense value of using NLP principles in my coaching practice. I found a fantastic course and worked intensively to become a Certified Practitioner of NLP, a Certified NLP Coach, and a Certified Practitioner of Timeline Therapy. This investment in myself has equipped me with the skills needed to elevate my coaching from a 6 out of 10 to a 10 out of 10. Of course, it takes practice, so I'd say I'm currently around an 8 out of 10 and working hard to improve.

Alongside my consultancy business, I decided to launch a coaching venture that focuses on helping men rediscover their purpose in life and shed any limiting beliefs that may be holding them back. Just as my coach had helped me, I felt a powerful desire to extend that support to others.

The GROW Model

When I first encountered coaching training, we used a model called GROW. Interestingly, the GROW model is also a fundamental component of NLP coaching.

The GROW model is a fantastic framework for coaching that really helps guide goal setting and conversations.

Goal: Start by clearly defining what you want to achieve. It's helpful to make the goal specific and something you can track along the way.

Reality: Take an honest look at where you are right now. This means understanding your current position in relation to the goal, thinking about the challenges you face, the resources you have, and any obstacles that might come up.

Options: Explore diverse ways you could move forward. Think about various strategies or actions you could take, considering the benefits and drawbacks of each one.

Will (or Way Forward): Choose the specific steps you're going to take. This is about making a commitment to the actions that will move you closer to your goal, along with setting a timeline to keep things moving.

The beauty of the GROW model is that it encourages self-reflection and helps with problem-solving skills, making it a really valuable tool for coaching and personal development.

My Superstar Coach

I want to finish this section by sharing my thoughts on the best coach I've ever had. To my knowledge, he doesn't have any formal coaching qualifications. Like me, he benefited from having his own coach during that same leadership programme I mentioned earlier. While I did notice a slight shift in his approach during his own personal development journey, it didn't significantly change how he had always coached me.

He has a remarkable ability to use silence to draw out deeper thoughts. It's likely a natural talent rather than something he learned. Many people tend to jump in too quickly with their opinions, often leaning more towards mentoring than coaching. But when you truly need help with a challenge, you require a coach - someone who can help you unpack a problem, and that often involves embracing silence.

When he saw I was struggling or hadn't fully explored a solution, he would simply remain silent, looking at me for what felt like an eternity - though it was probably just a couple of seconds. Then he'd ask questions like, "So what else could you do about it?" or "Why do you think you felt that way?" or "When did you first believe you couldn't do that?"

From him, I learned that there's always at least one more question to ask before someone can truly dig into a problem. That's my advice to you: even when it seems like someone has explored all angles, as a coach, use silence to find that one question that pushes your coachee deeper.

Thankfully, I'm still in touch with him all these years later. We still make time to meet up for a few beers once a quarter, helping each other navigate life's challenges with our own coaching styles.

Conclusion

This section is all about doing right by your team, ensuring they have fulfilling, successful careers. In those early days, mentorship will be like a rock for them, providing stability and support. But soon after, they'll need a continual stretch – that bit of challenge – to keep growing. One-on-one coaching is exactly what will help them develop further, and as a sales leader, it's your responsibility to make sure they get the attention they need.

Now, while it would be fantastic if you pursued a formal coaching qualification, you don't need to wait for that to start making a difference. Even if you stick to the simple principles we've already covered in this lesson, you'll begin to see progress. The key? *Stop telling and start asking* – it's really as simple as that.

Please don't feel you need a long list of pre-prepared questions for each coaching session either. Start small. Ask one or two good, open-ended questions to get the conversation going and build from there. You'd be surprised what insights come up when you embrace silence and use it as your secret weapon. Try it – you might be amazed at what your team brings to the surface when given the space to think.

Lesson 14: System Usage

At the start of this book, I mentioned that sales leadership revolves around people, process, and systems - each working together to drive success. So, as we begin to explore system usage and how salespeople interact with these tools, it's crucial to take a holistic approach to the best way forward.

When I first started in sales all those years ago, the focus was primarily on CRM systems. Today, however, salespeople interact with a wide range of systems on a daily basis, some of which are shown below.

CRM System: This is where you keep everything organised when it comes to your customers. It tracks all interactions, like emails and meetings, and helps you see where each deal is in the sales process. By having all the details in one place, you can follow up smoothly and keep your relationships strong.

Email Marketing Platform: This tool makes it easier to stay in touch with your customers through targeted email campaigns. Whether it's sending newsletters, offers, or updates, you can personalise your messages and track how people are responding. It helps you stay connected with your audience in a way that feels natural.

Sales Enablement Tools: These tools give your sales team everything they need to do their job well - things like brochures, case studies, or training guides. Having quick access to this information means they can focus on meaningful conversations with customers instead of searching for materials or answers.

Lead Generation Software: This software quietly works in the background to find new potential customers for you. It collects leads from various places, like your website or social media, and helps you gently guide them through the sales process until they're ready to make a decision.

E-commerce Platform: If you sell online, this platform takes care of things like managing your product listings, handling customer orders, and processing payments. It makes running your online store more straightforward, so you can focus on serving your customers.

Proposal and Quotation Software: This tool helps you send out quotes and proposals in a more organised way. You can use templates and automation to create professional documents quickly, making it easier to keep track of what you've sent and follow up when needed.

Accounting Software: This system quietly manages your finances behind the scenes, tracking transactions and helping with invoicing. It gives you peace of mind by keeping everything in order and helping with financial reports when you need them.

Communication Tools: These tools bring together all your ways of communicating, whether it's messaging, video calls, or phone systems. Everything is in one place, which makes it easier to collaborate with your team and respond to clients quickly.

Analytics and Reporting Tools: These tools help you understand how your business is doing by tracking key numbers like sales and customer trends. They make it easier to see what's working and where you might want to make adjustments.

Social Media Management Tools: Managing your social media accounts is simpler with these tools. You can plan and schedule posts, respond to messages, and see how people are interacting with your content, all from one place. It helps you stay engaged with your audience in a more thoughtful way.

Managing Adoption Pain

Before we get into the details, I want to take a step back - up to 35,000 feet - and look at this from the broadest possible perspective. When selecting any of the systems mentioned above (and others you may be considering), it's vital to return to that holistic approach: people, process, and systems. Ask yourself: *WHAT* do I want my people to do on a daily basis? *HOW* do I want them to do it (the process)? And *WHERE* should they do it (the system)?

The reason I emphasise this is that the number one challenge I hear from sales leaders' repeatedly is adoption. Phrases like: *"Yes, we implemented a new CRM system, but the sales adoption is terrible."* Or: *"We're pushing everything through the sales enablement platform to track engagement, but adoption is poor."* And perhaps: *"Only about 30% of quotes are logged in the quoting tool; most of the team are stuck in their old ways, so adoption rates are low."*

I bet you've heard similar statements in your business and will likely hear them again in the future. The problem is, unless you consider people, process, and systems as one integrated entity, any new system you introduce will just feel like an extra bolt-on - something people are forced to use rather than something that feels seamless and natural. And the root issue? Resistance to change.

From a sales perspective resistance to change is about the hesitation or refusal of your sales team to adopt new methods, processes, or tools that are introduced to improve their performance. This resistance can manifest in several ways, such as reluctance to use the recent technology, sticking to their outdated sales strategies, or being sceptical about changes to how they engage with these new ways.

Dealing With Change Resistance

To explain, let me tell you a quick story about one of my consulting clients. I'll mask the name of the company for obvious reasons! When I was brought in to start working with the sales team at this industrial manufacturing business, they seemed to have a solid foundation, or so I was told. They were good performers, consistently hitting their quarterly sales targets and building strong customer relationships. What more could you ask for? But, as with many sales teams, they'd fallen into the trap of relying on their old methods.

The company had just rolled out a new CRM system, and you could feel the resistance in the air when I began engaging with the team on their daily tasks. Some of the team simply refused to use it, while others begrudgingly updated the bare minimum and then continued working the way they always had - on dreaded Excel sheets.

It wasn't that they didn't want to do a good job. They did. But for them, the system felt like a hindrance, not help. I understood that feeling. After all, these were salespeople who had built their routines around what worked for them in the past. They knew their customers, had their own ways of organising leads, and felt that switching to a new system would just slow them down. They'd built years of relationships using certain techniques that were tailored to their personal style and introducing something new disrupted that flow.

There's a deep-rooted fear of the unknown in many salespeople when it comes to change. They worry the new tools will be difficult to learn, and that it'll take time away from actually selling. One of the team members confided in me, saying, "Paul, I just don't see how this CRM is going to help me hit my targets. It feels like more admin."

It's a valid concern. When you've been hitting your targets month on month, quarter on quarter, year after year, you're bound to feel comfortable with the way you work. If the current approach delivers results, why change? And that's where the problem lies. This resistance isn't about laziness – the biggest challenge comes from the risk in the mind of that salesperson. The risk that the new system might slow them down, add complexity, or worse, cost them a sale.

But what they often don't see is the bigger picture. These changes are introduced for a reason. A new CRM, for example, might feel like a headache at first, but it's designed to make their life easier in the long run, streamline their process, and give them insights they couldn't get before. The issue is, they don't always feel the benefits right away. And when you're in sales, if you don't see results quickly, it's easy to write it off as a waste of time.

So, what do you do in these situations? How do you move a team past that resistance? For me, it's about showing them the 'why' behind the change. What's in it for them - the people. Remember People, Process, and Systems. I'll sit down with them and explain how, if used correctly, this new tool will help them be more efficient, how it'll give them back time in the long run, and how it can provide a clearer view of their pipeline and customers. But it doesn't stop at talking;

you have to guide them through it. Training is key. Showing them how it integrates into their day-to-day processes, how it can make their work easier.

A key element is leadership. If you want your sales team to embrace new systems or processes, they have to see that you're fully behind it as well. That means leading by example. If you're not using the system yourself, it sends the message that it's not really essential, and the team will pick up on that.

This comes down to helping them understand why it matters and giving them the tools and support they need to succeed with it. Resistance to change is natural in sales. Our job as leaders is to break through that wall.

Always Lead by Example

In one company I worked with we had a new CEO join to help take us to the next level of growth. Having learned to code back in his day, he was huge fan of all systems. He immediately began to get stuck into the CRM. From day one, he was crawling all over the system, hunting for insights on where we could accelerate. Nothing gets a sales leadership team and salespeople more engaged in a CRM than the CEO actively using it and asking questions about what he's seeing.

We already had decent adoption before he arrived, but there was room for improvement. That improvement came within a week. To a salesperson, seeing the CEO lead by example sends a powerful message: the system isn't just a flash-in-the-pan idea; it's here to stay and, more importantly, is central to how we do business.

Creating Sales Habits

Salespeople often build habits and routines around familiar practices that they feel have worked for them in the past. When change is introduced - whether it's a new CRM system, updated sales training, or shifting from in-person meetings to digital ones, as we all remember - it can disrupt these routines. Salespeople may fear that the novel approach will complicate their job, reduce their efficiency, or put their success at risk.

The underlying reasons for resistance often include:

Fear of the Unknown: Salespeople might feel uneasy about learning new tools or processes, worrying that it could be tricky, slow them down, or lead to mistakes. That uncertainty can make them hesitant to dive in.

Comfort with the Status Quo: When the current way of doing things has been working, it's natural for the sales team to wonder if there's really a need to change. They may feel comfortable sticking with what they know.

Lack of Perceived Benefit: If the salesperson doesn't clearly see how the change will make their job easier or improve their performance, they might not feel it's worth the effort to adopt something new.

Workload Concerns: With any change, there's usually a learning curve, which can feel like added work. If it takes time away from selling, it might seem more like a burden than a benefit at first.

Overcoming this resistance to change typically requires clear communication about the benefits to all, proper training, and support, as well as strong leadership that shows the value of the change in improving results.

Practical Advice

After completing your holistic review of People, Process, and Systems, and deciding to introduce a shiny new piece of sales technology, it's essential to consider how to support your team in adopting this 'exciting' new system. Your business is unique and may therefore require specific strategies, but here are some fundamental steps to help you get started:

Communicate the Vision: Keep everyone in the loop by regularly sharing the long-term vision for the system and how it supports the company's broader goals. This helps remind the team why the system matters and how it fits into the bigger picture.

Set Clear Goals: Outline specific, manageable objectives related to the new system so the team knows what success looks like. Having these clear goals helps everyone focus on what they're working towards.

Comprehensive and Tailored Training: Offer hands-on training sessions that cater to different learning styles. This way, everyone can learn at their own pace and feel more comfortable and confident using the new system.

Integrate into Daily Workflows: Demonstrate how the new system fits smoothly into existing workflows. When team members can see how it enhances what they're already doing, it's easier to embrace.

Create a Champion Network: Identify team members who are particularly enthusiastic and let them take on the role of system champions. They can help others along the way and keep the energy positive.

Leadership Involvement: Encourage leaders to actively use the system and share their experiences. This sends a strong message about its value and encourages others to get on board.

Highlight Quick Wins: Share early successes that show how the system is making a difference. These small victories can help build confidence and keep the team motivated.

Ongoing Support: Make sure the team has access to helpful resources, whether it's a dedicated helpdesk, FAQs, or training materials. This way, they can easily get answers when they run into questions.

Incorporate Feedback: Repeatedly ask for feedback from the team about how the system is working for them. Listening to their input and adjusting helps improve the experience for everyone.

Conclusion

The moral of this story is that resistance to change in sales often stems from uncertainty and a fear of disruption. There's nothing more disruptive to a salesperson's flow than having to adopt a new system. However, when leaders take the initiative to actively demonstrate its value - addressing the "what's in it for me" concern - it can help break down that resistance.

Salespeople often need to see how a change will benefit them personally before they feel comfortable with it. Clear communication, steady support, and sharing real examples of where the new system is working well can help the team ease into new processes. When change is approached with confidence and transparency, it can feel less like a risk and more like a positive step forward.

Lesson 15: Data and Reporting

I'm going to let you in on something that's bothered me throughout my entire sales career: data and reporting. For years, I've been sent enormous files filled with every conceivable piece of data imaginable. Data analysts, excited by numbers and eager to highlight their skills, present these sprawling reports to the leadership team. They break them down by Global, Region, Country, Cluster, Territory, and even down to the individual salesperson. In theory, these reports are supposed to give you a complete picture of what's happening across the business.

You've probably heard of dyslexia. A quick Google search defines it as a specific learning difficulty that affects reading, writing, and spelling. It relates to challenges with processing language, making it hard to recognise words and understand written material. Now, while this description focuses on language, I'm convinced there's a number-based equivalent - and if it exists, I'm pretty sure I've got it. The thought of opening another complex spreadsheet filled with numbers and calculations honestly fills me with dread. And I know I'm not alone - many salespeople I've worked with feel the same. We don't want to sift through endless data; we just want to know what it means for us.

In fact, what salespeople really need is what I like to call Actionable Intelligence - the real AI for salespeople. It's about being presented with clear, actionable insights that enable them to make informed decisions, rather than drowning in a sea of data. Actionable Intelligence provides targeted information tailored to their specific sales goals, highlighting trends and opportunities.

You might remember back in Lesson 8 when I used the analogy of a pilot flying a plane. A cockpit is filled with hundreds of buttons, dials, and screens. How could anyone possibly keep track of them all? The truth is most are only used in specific situations. In reality, the pilot focuses on just a few key instruments to keep the plane flying smoothly.

Sales is much the same. There's data everywhere, endless reports, and countless targets to hit. It's easy to feel overwhelmed. But just like flying, the key is focusing on the most important instruments - the right AI.

Actionable Intelligence

In sales, I often feel things can become overcomplicated due to the sheer amount of data. I've personally spent hours, sometimes days, sifting through different data sources just to find the answers I needed. While data can certainly provide one perspective, it's essential to validate those findings by engaging with your team and customers. Reflecting on my time studying business research methods during my MBA, this would fall into the categories of quantitative and qualitative data. What is the data telling me (quantitative). What are the customers saying (qualitative).

Now, imagine how complex this process becomes if you're doing it every single day. And in reality, if you're guiding a sales team, you should be reviewing the data daily. But much like flying an aircraft, you need to be cautious not to overwhelm yourself or, more importantly, your team. That's why I'm a fan of Actionable Intelligence - a focused set of numbers chosen to provide the right level of insight. You'll know when to push harder, ease off, or change course.

Think of it this way: you're the pilot of your own plane, and that plane represents your sales results. What would be the five key dials you'd need to check every day to ensure you're heading in the right direction? It's really that simple. Select five relevant data points and live by them every day.

Of course, choosing these key metrics is probably the hardest part. But once you've settled on them, and they're delivering actionable intelligence to your team, you'll be "flying high" - pardon the pun.

Introducing the Five Dials Concept

Please do take the time to work with your team to define what your five key dials should be for your business. However, I thought it might be helpful to share something I've recently implemented during a consulting assignment with an industrial software company. Much of their sales efforts are focused on securing new business, while a separate team handles the customer success part, once the client is onboarded with the software solution.

The dials for the customer success team will naturally be different, and we'll get to those in a moment, but here's what we put in place for the new business team.

New Business Team

Pipeline Health: This shows the volume, value, and velocity of deals in the pipeline. It's important to track how many opportunities are at each stage, the potential revenue they bring, and how fast they're progressing. Are deals getting stuck, or are they moving along nicely? This dial gives us a clear picture of what's in play and helps us prioritise where to focus our efforts.

Win Rate: This is all about the percentage of deals won versus lost. By keeping an eye on this, we can see how well we're converting opportunities into sales. If win rates start to slip, it's a sign we need to dig deeper - maybe offer more coaching, fine-tune the sales process, or address any recurring customer objections.

Average Deal Size: This dial tracks the average value of each deal we close. Are we consistently bringing in high-value deals, or is the size shrinking? Monitoring this helps us gauge whether our value proposition is landing and if the team is targeting the right customers or deals.

Sales Cycle Length: This shows how long, on average, it's taking to close a deal. If the sales cycle starts to drag out, it might indicate we're hitting more resistance, the market's shifting, or there are bottlenecks in the process. A shorter sales cycle means we're moving deals along quickly and freeing up time to pursue new opportunities.

Customer Engagement / Activity: This measures how often the team is interacting with prospects and customers - whether that's meetings, calls, or emails. High engagement levels usually drive better results, while low engagement suggests the team needs to refocus or re-energise their outreach efforts.

Hopefully, you can see that each of these reporting metrics, or dials, is actionable - nothing is measured just for the sake of it. Whether things are going well or not, each dial provides a clear opportunity for intervention to help improve the current situation.

Now, let's dive into the five key dials for the customer success team. This team is responsible for looking after the customer once they've gone live with the software solution.

Their focus is on ensuring the customer maximises the value of the solution and becomes a long-term advocate for the business and what it delivers for them.

Customer Success Team

Customer Health Score: This dial gives us a real-time snapshot of customer satisfaction and engagement. It tracks key indicators like product usage, feedback, and any support tickets raised. A declining health score would signal that a customer might be at risk, giving the team time to step in and address any issues before they escalate.

Retention Rate: This dial shows how many customers we're keeping versus losing. High retention is always the goal, but a drop in this number would tell us to dive into why customers are leaving. Is it due to service gaps, unmet expectations, or something else? Keeping this dial in check ensures the long-term success.

Customer Lifetime Value (CLV): This measures the total revenue a customer is expected to bring in over the course of their relationship with the company. By tracking CLV, we can identify high-value customers and focus on maximising their satisfaction, while also spotting opportunities for upselling or cross-selling.

Time to Resolution: This tracks how quickly the team resolves customer issues or queries. The faster we can resolve problems, the happier the customer. If resolution times start creeping up, it's a sign that the team may need extra support, process improvements, or additional resources to keep customers satisfied.

Customer Feedback & NPS (Net Promoter Score): This measures customer sentiment through surveys and direct feedback. NPS is a fantastic way to gauge loyalty by asking customers how likely they are to recommend your product or service. Negative feedback would indicate we need to dig deeper to improve customer experience, while positive feedback helps identify what's working well.

Once again, each dial is actionable. Whether things are trending up or down, there's always an opportunity to take action and push for improvement.

The key takeaway from having these five dials - or four or six, depending on your specific needs - is to keep things simple and actionable. This ensures your team has absolute clarity on the goals and knows exactly how to achieve them.

Monthly Report Nonsense

Before we wrap up this section, I'd like to address the topic of reporting - specifically, the Monthly Report. You've seen it before, haven't you? It's the last day of the month, and every salesperson is scrambling to submit their report to the sales manager. They dread the task, unsure if anyone even reads it, and often feel it's a waste of their time. The reports tend to be vague and fluffy, quickly becoming a tick-box exercise that merely checks if someone has submitted their report on time.

The challenge arises when the sales manager has to compile their report for upper management. This requires a special skill set to sift through all the individual reports and extract the most relevant points worthy of the CEO's attention - if it even gets reviewed.

If you have the right five dials in place for your business, it's time to eliminate the monthly reporting cycle altogether. Here's my advice: stop it - right now - and don't let it return.

Instead, implement a **Monthly Health Check** with your team. Use the qualitative data from the dials and gather quantitative feedback during the discussion. Ensure that the team has access to the data beforehand and schedule a monthly call to review the month's results. Discuss the highs, the lows, and any changes that may need to be implemented. Each salesperson should be able to articulate their story of the month in just a couple of minutes, allowing you to capture and assign any necessary actions across the team.

If you do need to provide a report for upper management, I recommend inviting senior leaders to attend your call so they can hear the insights directly. If that's not possible, you can provide a high-level commentary on the five dials' performance, based on the quantitative feedback gathered during the Health Check meeting. This approach streamlines your reporting cycle and helps build a culture of collaboration and accountability.

Conclusion

My closing message for this lesson is straightforward. When analysing data and reporting, always consider why you're undertaking this task, what your goals are, and what changes you hope to see. Focus on delivering **Actionable Intelligence** to your team, ensuring every insight leads to meaningful progress.

CUSTOMER SUCCESS

Lesson 16: Customer Onboarding

We've reached a key turning point in this book. Up until now, we've focused on how we develop our people, processes, and systems to win new clients. Now, it's time to shift our attention to what comes next - how we establish and grow a strong relationship with our new customers. In the last lesson, I briefly touched on the idea of a customer success team, and this section dives deeper into that concept. While having a dedicated customer success team might seem like a luxury for many businesses, the principles behind it are valuable, and we can adapt them to suit our needs. To kick off this journey, we're starting with the critical first step: onboarding.

Onboarding a customer is a lot like bringing a new team member into your business, as we discussed in Lesson 12 on Induction and Onboarding. Once a client agrees to the partnership, the next step is to ensure they smoothly integrate into your processes and understand how your business operates. It's about setting the right tone from the beginning, making sure they feel supported and confident as they navigate those early stages. Just as you would with a new employee, you want your customers to feel like they belong, confident they've made the right decision. And, as we'll explore in later lessons, investing time and effort into this early stage can lead to stronger customer advocacy - and potentially, some excellent referrals.

Think of it like a well-structured induction. When a new employee joins your team, you don't just drop them in at the deep end. You introduce them to the tools, systems, and people they'll be working with. You take time to explain the culture and help them see how they fit into the bigger picture. The same logic applies to your customers. By carefully onboarding them, you're laying the groundwork for success. You're showing them what to expect, how you'll support them, and what they can do to make the most out of the relationship.

A smooth onboarding process builds trust from day one. It shows that you care about the details and are committed to building a long-term relationship. Just like with a new employee, the better you onboard your customers, the quicker they'll settle in and start delivering value - not just for themselves, but for your business too.

B2C Strategies for B2B Success

In this book, we've focused a lot on B2B practices, but when it comes to managing customers, there's a lot we can learn from the way we interact with businesses in our personal lives. I'm sure you've used Amazon or Apple and experienced how they make you feel as a customer -the ease of use, the simplicity of everything falling into place without drama - and you've probably even thought, "Why can't we do that here?"

I want to share a story about a recent household utility switch I made. The company offers a range of services including energy (gas and electricity), mobile SIMs, broadband, and even insurance products. Their whole proposition is centred around convenience, with one provider offering all these services under one relationship and one bill. When you're consolidating utilities in this way, it requires confidence that the company will handle everything smoothly and ensure a successful experience.

I was approached by a consultant from this company, and she too was based in Peterborough, where I live. At first, I was quite apprehensive. Why? Because I'd been with the same energy company for 14 years, the same mobile provider for 12, and the same broadband supplier for 9. You might think I'd been missing out on better deals by not switching, and perhaps I had. But rest assured, I'd negotiated with my providers every time my contract was up, making sure I felt comfortable that I got the best possible deal. What really held me back was the thought of hassle, and more so, the risk. What if I switched broadband and ended up without service for a few days? What if my new SIM wasn't activated, and I missed an important call about a new consultancy project? These were genuine concerns, and I'd managed fine for this long, so why take the risk now?

Her approach wasn't what I expected. Instead of pushing me to sign up, she focused on my outcomes - on customer success. She reviewed my current suppliers and was upfront about where I could save money and where I couldn't. For example, the energy switch was a simple decision. They had a fantastic fixed-price tariff that was better than anything else on the market at the time. By consolidating all the family's mobile SIMs into one provider, there were also significant savings to be had. However, my broadband contract still had 12 months left. While their offer had a slight saving over my current provider, the cancellation fees would outweigh any benefits. She was focused on saving me money and making sure I saw clear value from the outset.

She then showed me the app I'd be using to manage my contracts and bills, and I was immediately impressed. It was user-friendly, simple to navigate, and everything was easy to find. She explained how the customer service team operated, how I could reach out if something went wrong, and what steps to take if I needed to escalate an issue. Again, she was thinking about my success before I even signed up.

After agreeing to the terms and conditions, I instantly received all the information I needed via text and email. From setting up the app to understanding the billing cycles, everything was seamless. I even received clear instructions on how to switch the phones over, and from that moment, the customer success journey shifted into high gear.

Like many businesses today, this company relies heavily on automated communications. However, what sets them apart - and why I'm sharing this story as a B2C success example - is the personal touch from their consultants. On day one, she called to let me know that all the processes had begun and that I would be receiving various emails over the next 24-48 hours with updates. She informed me that my three new SIMs had been ordered and would be shipped that day. She even explained that, because I went live on the 20th of the month, I wouldn't receive a bill at the end of the month as usual. Instead, my first bill would include a part-month charge the following month. Everything was running smoothly, and I felt reassured.

The next day, she called again to check in. "Have you received your new SIMs, and do you have your PAC codes from your old provider?" she asked. I had. "Great," she replied, "Do you need help with the process, or would you like me to walk you through one phone first?" I felt confident following the simple instructions, so I declined, but I appreciated the offer. "Not a problem," she said. "Call if you get stuck." And with that, I switched all the phones over without a problem.

The following day, she sent a text reminding me to take a picture of my gas and electricity meter readings just in case there were any disputes with my previous supplier. Although the smart meter should take care of it, she knew I was a bit nervous and wanted to provide that extra safeguard just in case something went wrong.

Within a few days, everything had switched over - our gas and electricity were now with my new provider, and all our phones were working as expected. The app was brilliant. I could access everything I needed, see the upcoming billing cycle, and it was all so easy to manage. Job done, or so I thought.

But what really sets this business apart is how they continue the customer success journey long after the initial switch. A few days later, my consultant called again to check that everything was working as expected and to make sure I was happy with the service so far. Everything was working perfectly, of course, and I told her as much.

A couple of weeks later, she reached out once more, this time with some unexpected, good news. She informed me that the standard variable tariff was about to rise, which meant the fixed-price deal I had secured would result in even greater savings than we had originally calculated. This was just another example of how the company, and consultants in particular, understood what was important to me- delivering real value and making sure I continued to see the benefits long after the switch.

This whole experience was a great reminder of what customer success truly looks like. It's not just about securing the initial deal; it's about continuing to deliver value, staying in touch, and making sure the customer feels supported every step of the way. They did exactly that. The switch was the start of a relationship that was built on trust, transparency, and a commitment to ensuring I was happy and saving money. That's the essence of true customer success.

B2B Customer Success

At a previous employer of mine we had a dedicated customer success team that played a crucial role in onboarding new customers into the inner workings of the company. Much like in the utilities example I shared earlier, the customer success team engaged with prospective clients early on, working with them long before any deal was agreed. This was because, much like with my energy switch, clients needed to trust what they were signing up for - both in terms of tangible and intangible value.

When I reflect on the deals I won while there, I can confidently say that our success came from this brilliant customer success approach. Of course, every company wants to secure the business - that's a given - but what we truly focused on was building long-term partnerships. This involved laying strong foundations from the very start, ensuring the relationship could extend well into the future.

We asked key questions early: Who would be using the software platform? What specific use cases do you want to address? How will it integrate into your existing tech stack? Where will the data come from, and where will the output go? What reporting cycles are required? How will your commercial team need to adjust to adopt this modern technology? What training will be necessary? What metrics matter most to the C-suite, and what's essential for daily operations? What changes would you like to see after 3 months, 6 months, or a year? Plus, many more!

These details were critical, and nothing was left unexamined. Our aim was for the customer to see value from the very first day their application went live. The benefits needed to be clear, and the return on investment had to be undeniable.

Now, this level of onboarding is elite. It's highly detailed and customised, but that doesn't mean you can't apply some of these principles to your own business, regardless of its size or industry. Even if your operations are more transactional, I'm certain there are a couple of areas where you could enhance the onboarding experience for your customers. Whether it's with more preparation or a greater focus on their long-term success, there are always improvements to be made.

With that in mind, I've put together a mid-level approach that I think would be practical for most businesses. These steps don't require an entire customer success department, but they do require a shift in thinking. Take a look at the following steps and consider how you might implement some - or all - of these ideas in your own business, even with a bit of customisation:

Provide a Personalised Welcome Package: As soon as the agreement is signed, send a personalised welcome package that includes all essential information about the partnership. This could include a welcome letter, key contacts, a detailed overview of the services or products they've signed up for, and clear next steps. Personalising this package helps set a positive tone and reassures the client that you're invested in their success from day one.

Schedule an Onboarding Call or Meeting: Arrange a structured onboarding call or meeting to introduce the key members of your team who will be working with the client.

During this session, outline what they can expect, review the project or service timeline, and address any questions. This creates transparency and aligns expectations, ensuring the client feels supported from the start.

Create a Step-by-Step Guide: Offer the client a step-by-step onboarding guide that explains the processes they need to follow. Whether it's using your product, navigating your systems, or understanding communication channels, a simple, well-organised guide can ease the transition. You could also include instructional videos, FAQs, or even a dedicated points of contact for specific queries.

Assign a Dedicated Account Manager: Give the client one main point of contact for any issues or questions. A dedicated account manager builds a personal connection, ensuring the client feels supported throughout their journey. The account manager should check in regularly, not just during the onboarding phase but beyond, to ensure everything is running smoothly.

Set Clear Goals and Regular Check-ins: Early in the relationship, define clear, measurable goals that align with the client's expectations. Schedule regular check-ins to discuss progress, review KPIs, and adjust plans if needed. This proactive approach demonstrates your commitment to their success and helps catch any issues before they become problems.

Conclusion

Everything we've covered in this onboarding lesson lays a strong foundation for the upcoming lessons. These initial steps will help the relationship grow and flourish as the days, weeks, and months progress.

Getting the onboarding process right is key to establishing strong, long-lasting relationships with your new customers. By prioritising their success from the very beginning, you create an atmosphere where customers feel valued and supported. This sets a solid foundation for future collaboration. Ultimately, investing time and effort in onboarding helps nurture loyalty and advocacy, paving the way for mutual success.

Lesson 17: Customer Feedback

Have you ever stopped to think about how your customers truly feel about your products or services? It's tempting to believe you've got it all figured out, particularly when things appear to be going well. But I've found over the years that some of the best insights - the ones that can drive real growth - come directly from customers themselves.

I think there's something about customer feedback that's often overlooked in a business strategy. In many ways, it's a direct hotline to the truth about how well you're meeting their needs. We all have good intentions when we create something, whether it's a product, service, or new approach, but intentions and outcomes don't always align. That's why I believe you should proactively seek out customer feedback at every opportunity.

Customer feedback acts like a mirror, showing you exactly what's working and where there's room for improvement. When I work with companies struggling to break through certain performance barriers, it's often feedback from the end-users that shines the light on what's really holding them back. You can have all the internal data in the world, but sometimes the simplest comments from customers are what unlocks that next level of performance.

Think about it - if you don't ask the people using your product or service what their experience is like, how will you know what needs tweaking? I've seen time and time again how small adjustments, based on customer input, can have a huge impact on satisfaction and retention. It might be something as simple as changing a process or offering an additional feature. But you won't know until you ask.

I think there's a strong connection between seeking feedback and building loyalty. People want to feel heard, and when you actively listen to your customers and take their input seriously, it builds trust. It shows that you genuinely care about their experience, which can make all the difference in whether they continue to buy.

In my experience, businesses that take feedback onboard and make visible changes tend to create stronger, longer-lasting relationships with their customers. This, in turn, leads to higher levels of customer retention, which is far more valuable than constantly chasing new business.

Innovation Comes from Listening

Sometimes, the next big idea or breakthrough feature is sitting right in front of you - tucked away in the feedback from your customers. It's easy to forget just how much innovation can come directly from them. They're the ones using your products or services in real-world situations, and their insights are often more valuable than we realise.

At a former company, we ran a growth accelerator programme that aimed to generate new business through fresh ideas and innovation. What struck me was that every idea came from the customers themselves. By focusing on their pain points and collaborating with cross-functional teams, we found new ways to solve their challenges. It brought a renewed sense of energy and direction to the business. And that's the real power of customer feedback - it can give you an entirely new perspective, one you might not have seen otherwise.

Dealing with Negative Experiences

One of the biggest risks any business faces is having dissatisfied customers who feel like they're not being listened to. It's when customers feel ignored that they're most likely to vent their frustrations, and that can quickly snowball if left unchecked. In my experience, proactively asking for feedback and addressing issues before they escalate can save you a lot of headaches down the road.

This approach probably stems from my early days when I was working in my territory role. The level of service our customers received was always incredibly high. It was something that really set us apart from the competition.

Because the service was so dependable, customers were quick to point out when things did go wrong – and those moments really stuck with you because they were so rare. I used to make a point of checking the system before heading out to meet a customer, just to see if there had been any hiccups with their deliveries. Then, during my visit, I'd ask, "How have your deliveries been this past month?" That's when I'd hear, "Oh, Paul, I'm glad you asked. There was this one order..."

Ah, the frustration! But that was my opportunity to fix it before it became a bigger issue. I'd respond, "I'm sure we can do something to stop that from happening again. Let me speak to the operations team on your behalf." And then, almost every time, they'd add, "But the other 200 orders were fine, it was just that one small problem."

That's the thing – it's always better to have those uncomfortable conversations directly with your customers, rather than letting them simmer. By seeking feedback early and often, you not only resolve issues quickly and quietly but also get the chance to highlight the positives in the relationship. It keeps the focus on the overall success while showing that you're dedicated to improving their experience.

Keeping Your Customers Happy

There's a lot of talk about customer churn these days – the idea that if people aren't happy, they'll leave. With so much choice out there, it's no surprise that this happens. But what often gets overlooked is that many of the reasons customers walk away are entirely preventable. I genuinely believe that if businesses took the time to regularly check in with their customers – whether it's through a conversation, surveys, polls, or forums – they'd see a significant reduction in churn.

When you actively engage with customers and show a genuine interest in improving their experience, it makes them feel involved. And when they feel like they have a stake in your business, they're far less likely to look elsewhere. It's that sense of investment that can make all the difference.

Back in my early days in sales, I saw firsthand how just a simple check-in could change the dynamic. By asking customers directly about their experience, I got ahead of potential problems and strengthened my relationships. The same principle applies whether you're doing it face-to-face, as I did, or using surveys or polls. It's all about showing that you care about what they think and that their feedback is crucial to you.

I also believe that one of the biggest benefits of engaging with your customers is the confidence it gives you in your decision-making. When you're making decisions based solely on internal assumptions or perspectives, it's easy to second-guess yourself. Are you really making the right call?

But when you incorporate customer feedback, you're grounding your choices in real-world data. It's no longer a guess; it's an informed decision based on the people who matter most – your customers.

I've seen this time and again, especially through the growth accelerator programmes I've been part of. When you're uncertain about a new direction or idea, validating those plans with customer feedback gives you the reassurance you need. There's something incredibly reassuring about knowing the changes you're implementing are based on the actual experiences and needs of the people who use your products or services daily.

In the end, customer feedback should be about creating a partnership with your customers, showing them that their input shapes the future of your business. And when you build that connection, you can build long-term loyalty.

My Most Memorable Experience

In the B2C world, you'll notice that feedback is often captured digitally. When you're dealing with such large volumes of customers, it's really the only practical way to manage it. However, in B2B, it's different – you need to find ways to speak directly to your customers, as I've highlighted through earlier examples. One of the most impactful and memorable experiences I had in gathering customer feedback was during my time in the world of office products. This employer was an office products wholesaler. I say "was" because, unfortunately, they've recently had to close down their operations.

They had a long-standing history, serving office product resellers for over 200 years – yes, 200 years. It was a brilliant business model. Office products resellers could focus on selling to their customers using a catalogue, which they could brand as their own – essentially a white-labelling system. The wholesaler managed the logistics, keeping thousands of products in stock and dispatching them overnight to their dealer partners by 6 a.m. That meant the resellers could make local deliveries the very next morning. It was an incredibly efficient operation.

But as you can imagine, since the pandemic there's been a huge decline in the number of people working in physical office spaces, resulting in a significant reduction in demand for office products. This trend had been impacting the industry for years, and sadly, it eventually caught up with them.

In the relatively brief period, I worked in the business, there was one area where they excelled compared to other businesses I've worked with: proactively seeking out customer feedback, or, in this industry, dealer feedback. Once a quarter, the senior team would meet with the Dealer Advisory Forum (DAF), which consisted of six business owners from office products dealerships. These meetings were invaluable for sharing insights into market challenges, exploring new opportunities, and discussing how we could better support their needs.

During these sessions, we would introduce new product lines to the DAF first, assessing their market viability at a local level. We'd also explore collaborative marketing campaigns to help generate new business and even brainstorm ways to improve logistics associated with transportation - from the warehouse to the dealers' premises and then onward to the end customer. This approach allowed us to hear firsthand what additional support these businesses needed to help them grow.

To keep things fresh and relevant, we also brought in six new members to the DAF each year. This ensured we were constantly gathering new intelligence, allowing us to refine and improve everything we did for our customers – the office products dealers. It was a dynamic way to stay connected with the market and address the evolving needs of our partners.

Conclusion

Customer feedback is an invaluable resource that can significantly drive business growth, enhance customer satisfaction, and build lasting loyalty. By actively seeking out feedback from your customers, you will gain valuable insights into their needs, preferences, and pain points. This enables you to make informed decisions that truly reflect their expectations. Building this connection demonstrates to your customers that their voices matter to you.

To maximise the benefits of this feedback, it's essential to adopt a structured approach. First, establish multiple channels for gathering insights - whether through surveys, focus groups, or direct conversations (which has always been my preference). Regardless of the method you choose, make it clear that you're committed to acting on their feedback, and be transparent about how their input shapes your business decisions.

Once you've collected the feedback, dedicate time to analyse and prioritise the insights. Look for common themes and focus on areas that will have the most significant impact on the customer experience. Implement changes based on this feedback, and don't forget to communicate the outcomes to your customers, reinforcing their role in the improvement process.

Finally, treat feedback as an ongoing conversation rather than a one-off task - much like my approach with customers when in sales or through the Dealer Advisory Forums. Regularly check in with customers and be ready to adjust your strategies as their needs evolve.

Lesson 18: Customer Relationship Management

As odd as this may sound, it's absolutely true - I love CRM systems. Everything about them fills me with joy. The ability to have a single view of everything related to a customer relationship is such a valuable asset, isn't it? With just a quick search or the click of a button, you can find account order history, contact interactions, revenue, and profit data, and so much more. Gone are the days of rummaging through different spreadsheets, logging into various platforms, or asking 'Bob' if he remembers who he last spoke to at Acme Plc back in 2008.

What's even better is how accessible and user-friendly this technology has become. I currently use HubSpot for my consultancy business and have been a heavy user of Salesforce in the past. Both platforms are incredibly easy to set up, manage, and use - so much so that even I can do it! When setting up my consultancy, I wanted my pipeline to flow exactly as described in Lesson 4. After navigating to the right menu, I could easily add or remove stages, rename them, and incorporate extra features like confidence percentages. Uploading my prospects from my Excel start-up sheet was a breeze, and as they converted into customers, I continued the engagement using notes, tasks, and activity tracking - all within the system.

I remember using some of those old on-premise CRM systems before cloud-based applications became widespread. Any minor change required a developer, a formal change request, and then had to be prioritised alongside all other IT tasks. It took ages. I once needed to check if an order was placed after a campaign was sent to a customer. The process involved a lot of talk about "fuzzy logic" - whatever that is - yet even after implementation, the results weren't always accurate. Nowadays, your CRM can link seamlessly with your marketing activities and ordering systems, connecting everything together so that these kinds of checks are effortless and dependable.

So, if it's now easy to set up, use, and highly accurate, why do some salespeople still resist using these systems? Well, it comes down to that word: "SYSTEMS." As I mentioned earlier in this book, success in sales comes from the right combination of PEOPLE, PROCESS, and SYSTEMS. Too often, businesses implement a CRM system, expecting it to be a golden ticket that solves all their problems, without considering how to get their people to adopt it effectively. For a CRM to truly work, salespeople need to see its benefits and understand the process steps required to make it successful - for themselves, the company, and, ultimately, the customer.

In this lesson, we'll explore CRM from a people and process perspective. The technology is already there - what's crucial is how you integrate it with your team and your strategy.

When we think about CRM systems, it's easy to get caught up in the technology. The promise of seamless integration, instant access to customer data, and automation can sound like a dream for any sales team. But in my experience, the success happens not because of the technology itself, but because of the people using it. The CRM is just a tool - an important one, yes - but a tool, nonetheless. It's the people behind it, the ones building and nurturing relationships, who make all the difference.

So, what does that look like in practice? How do the best salespeople use a CRM system to enhance - not replace - their human connections? Let's explore some of the key behaviours that set top-performing salespeople apart when they interact with both their CRM and their customers.

Focusing on Relationships

At its core, sales is about relationships. Yes, there's a lot of data that comes with it, but data is just the foundation. The real work happens in those personal interactions between the salesperson and the customer. Great salespeople know this. When they use a CRM, they aren't just filling in fields or checking boxes as we've mentioned before - they're thinking about how the information in the system can help them deepen their relationship with the customer.

For example, a good CRM system can tell you when a customer's birthday is or remind you of the last time they placed an order. Which can be a little bland when used in isolation. But it's the salesperson's responsibility to turn that information into a meaningful interaction. Perhaps the customer mentioned during their last conversation that they were having trouble with a particular product. A great salesperson would use that detail to follow up, offer help, or suggest a solution - turning what could have been just another routine follow-up into a valuable, personalised touchpoint.

In this sense, the CRM is a tool that supports relationships, not the relationship itself. It helps salespeople stay organised, remember vital details, and ensure they're always one step ahead. But it's the salesperson's responsibility to empathise, listen, and respond in a way that feels personal and genuine.

Consistency is Key

Consistency is one of the most important qualities of a successful salesperson. Customers notice when you're reliable, when you follow through on your promises, and when you make an effort to stay in touch. Your CRM can help your salespeople stay organised and ensure that no customer gets forgotten, but again, it's the person using it who creates the real value.

Great salespeople use their CRM to manage their time effectively and ensure they're always on top of their tasks. But for me, consistency is about showing up in meaningful ways, repeatedly. Whether it's a quick email to check in, sharing a relevant article, or sending a personal note after a big order, the best salespeople will use the CRM to support their ability to be consistently engaged with their customers.

I'm a huge believer that consistency builds trust. When a customer knows they can rely on you to stay in touch and follow through on your commitments, it strengthens the relationship. The CRM makes this easier, of course, by reminding salespeople when it's time to reach out or follow up. But it's the thoughtfulness behind those interactions that really makes an impact.

Active Listening Skills

One of the most overlooked skills in sales is the ability to listen. And I don't just mean listening to what a customer is saying at the surface level - I'm talking about truly listening to understand what they need, what they're struggling with, and what their goals are. Remember when we talked about addressing pain points. Salespeople who master this skill are able to offer solutions that have real influence, because they're responding to the customer's specific needs.

A CRM can help salespeople keep track of customer conversations and remember key details, but it can't do the listening for them. That's where emotional intelligence comes in. Salespeople with high emotional intelligence are skilled at noticing subtle cues and understanding the underlying emotions behind a customer's words. They don't just take notes - they're engaged, asking thoughtful questions and really tuning in to what the customer is saying.

This kind of listening builds trust and rapport. It shows the customer that the salesperson genuinely cares about their success and isn't just trying to close a deal. And when it's paired with a well-maintained CRM, it becomes even more powerful. The system ensures that no details are lost, but it's the salesperson's ability to interpret and act on those details which makes the human connection.

Emotional Intelligence in Sales

Perhaps I should have written an entire lesson on Emotional Intelligence in sales – maybe one for a second book. But I feel that emotional intelligence is often the X-factor that sets great salespeople apart from good ones. It's the ability to navigate complex emotional dynamics, both with customers and within the sales team. A prominent level of emotional intelligence allows salespeople to adapt their approach based on the customer's mood, preferences, and communication style, making every interaction feel more personal and effective.

For example, a customer might express frustration about a delivery delay. A salesperson with strong emotional intelligence won't just apologise and move on - they'll professionally acknowledge the customer's feelings, empathise with their frustration, and work to find a solution that makes the customer feel heard and valued. The CRM helps by keeping track of these interactions, ensuring that future touchpoints can build on that empathy. But again, it's the person behind the system that brings the situation to life.

Collaborating with the Team

One of the wonderful things about modern CRMs is that they make it easy for teams to collaborate. Sales isn't a solo sport, even if it sometimes feels that way. Like most of us, salespeople depend on the support of their team, whether that's in the form of technical expertise, marketing insights, or simply sharing information about a customer.

A well-maintained CRM makes this kind of collaboration seamless. When everyone on the team is using the system effectively, it's easy to hand off a customer or bring in a colleague to help with a complex problem. But again, the system is just the enabler. It's the salesperson's willingness to share information, ask for help, and work together.

Collaboration is especially important in businesses where customer relationships can span multiple departments or teams. In these cases, the CRM becomes a central hub for all customer-related information, ensuring that everyone has access to the latest updates and insights. But the culture of collaboration within the team is what makes this work smoothly. I love it when I work with salespeople who are open, communicative, and willing to share information. Their actions really do contribute to a positive, team-oriented environment where the customer benefits from a more cohesive experience.

Trust and Transparency

We mentioned the word 'trust' earlier, and I feel this is at the heart of any successful customer relationship. When you are honest and transparent, you tend to build the strongest, longest-lasting connections with your customers. A CRM supports this by making it easy to track customer interactions and ensure that nothing falls through the cracks. But I really want to emphasise that it's the salesperson's commitment to being honest and transparent in the information that is entered which matters.

For example, if a product is delayed or a problem arises, that salesperson will be upfront about the issue, rather than trying to hide it. They'll communicate openly with the customer, explaining the situation and offering solutions. This kind of transparency builds trust, and trust is what keeps customers coming back, even when things don't go perfectly.

Embracing a Growth Mindset

When we get to our final lesson, we will discuss continuous improvement and growth mindset in greater detail. One thing I'm certain of is that sales is a constantly evolving field, and the best salespeople are those who embrace change and are always looking for ways to improve. A growth mindset - the belief that skills and abilities can be developed through effort and learning - should be an essential trait for all salespeople. In fact, it's a valuable quality for everyone, when you think about it.

Salespeople with a growth mindset don't see a CRM as a static tool. They're always looking for ways to use it more effectively, whether that's by refining their processes, learning new features, or using data to make smarter decisions. They view the CRM as a tool for continuous improvement, not just a system for logging what might be described as dull information.

For example, a salesperson with a growth mindset might regularly review their CRM data to find patterns in customer behaviour or track the effectiveness of their outreach efforts. They're using it to get better at what they do. This mindset of constant learning and improvement is what sets them apart from their peer group.

Conclusion

At the end of the day, a CRM system is only as good as the people using it. The real value of a CRM comes from the behaviours, skills, and mindsets of the salespeople who use it to enhance their relationships with customers. A CRM can help salespeople stay organised, track vital details, and collaborate with their team, but it's the human element that I really want you to take from this lesson.

Salespeople who focus on those key behavioural aspects, combined with a growth mindset are the ones who get the most out of their CRM. They understand that it's not the technology that makes the sale - it's the way they use it to support their relationships and deliver value to their customers.

In the end, it's the people behind the system who make the real impact.

Lesson 19: Customer Renewals

This lesson focuses on commercial contracts that are signed at the beginning of a trading relationship and set to expire after 1 year, 3 years, 5 years, and so on. It's a commitment to a partnership with a defined end date - a point where both parties can walk away. It sounds a bit harsh, doesn't it? After all, we've invested time in building the relationship, gaining a deep understanding of the customer's pain points and cultural needs. The proposal hit the mark, the pricing was spot on, and the roadmap for customer success resonated. We did pretty much everything right - otherwise, the customer wouldn't be ready to sign. Excellent job.

But if everything is going so well today, why are we already thinking about ending the relationship in 3 years? Why commit to an end when optimism is at its highest?

Well, when it comes to deciding whether or not to renew a contract, the thought process for both the customer and the seller is rarely as simple as "Do we continue or walk away?" *Just to clarify, when I use the term "seller," I'm referring to your company as the one providing a service to your customer.* There's often a lot more at play – emotions, business changes, and even a sense of whether the relationship has run its course. Let's take a closer look at the mindset of both the customer and the seller when it comes time to think about renewal.

The Customer's Perspective

For a customer, the first question they often ask is, "Is this still delivering the value we expected?" or "Have those customer success efforts really worked for us?" On the surface, it may seem like a simple evaluation, but there's usually much more happening beneath the surface.

Value for Money: Over time, customers naturally start weighing up the return on their investment. It's human nature. The service or product might have delivered early on, but has it continued to perform? "Are we still getting the same value we saw in the beginning?" If the answer feels like a 'no', they start questioning whether it's worth continuing.

Performance and Consistency: Even if things have mostly gone well, any slip-ups or issues that cropped up during the contract might linger in the customer's mind. It doesn't have to be a big problem – sometimes even small frustrations add up. "Has the service been dependable enough to carry us forward?" Customers value consistency, and if it's been lacking, that could be enough for them to consider alternatives.

Better Options: In the time since the contract was signed, the market may have moved on. New competitors might be offering more advanced solutions or better pricing. The customer starts wondering, "Could we be getting more for our money elsewhere?" The temptation to explore other options can sometimes outweigh the comfort of staying with what's familiar.

Internal Changes: There's also the matter of what's going on internally within the customer's business. Budgets may have tightened, priorities may have shifted, or new leadership could be pushing for a different direction. "Does this still fit with our business today?" What seemed essential when the contract was signed might no longer be as critical if their direction has changed.

Relationship Dynamics: Sometimes, it's not even about the product or service itself. The relationship between the customer and seller could have hit a rough patch. If the customer feels they're not being listened to or that the communication has become transactional, they might start thinking, "Are we really being heard?" Over time, this friction can create a sense of fatigue, where the customer feels like a fresh start is needed – even if the service itself is still good.

The Seller's Perspective

On the other side, as a seller, there's often a different set of considerations that come into play when renewal time approaches. While keeping the customer is always a priority, sellers also have to be realistic about whether continuing the relationship makes sense for them, too.

Customer Profitability: Not all customers are equally profitable. Over time, sellers might find that some customers are more resource-intensive than others. "Are we spending too much time and energy on this customer for the return we're getting?" If the relationship starts feeling unbalanced, it could lead to a decision not to push for renewal.

Strategic Fit: Sellers evolve, too. They may have shifted their focus or refined their offering since the contract was signed. "Does this customer still align with where we're heading as a business?" If the customer's needs no longer match what the seller is offering, then it might make sense to part ways, even if there hasn't been any major issue. It's about staying focused on the right fit.

Product Evolution: Sometimes, a seller's product or service has evolved in such a way that the customer's current needs no longer align. The seller might think, "Can we still add real value here, or has the customer's expectations or needs shifted?" This could be a mutual decision where both sides agree that the product has outgrown the customer's requirements.

Resource Strain: Sellers also have to think about how their resources are being used. If a customer has been particularly demanding or difficult to work with, the seller may start questioning whether it's worth the effort to keep the relationship going. "Is this customer stretching our team too thin?" It's a difficult call to make, but one that often comes up when a contract is nearing renewal.

Payment Issues: If the customer has been slow to pay or consistently trying to negotiate the price down, the seller may have concerns about the financial reliability of the relationship. "Is this customer worth the hassle when it comes to payments?" This can be the tipping point where the seller decides it's time to move on.

A Mutual Decision

Interestingly, there are times when both the customer and the seller independently reach the same conclusion: it's time to part ways. It's not always a negative decision - sometimes, both parties recognise that the relationship has simply run its course, and moving forward separately makes the most sense.

For the customer, this might be an opportunity to explore new services or products that align better with their current direction or evolving needs. On the seller's side, it could be a chance to refocus resources and build relationships with customers who fit more closely with their long-term strategy. It's simply a mutual decision to grow in different directions.

Now, let's play this out and transport ourselves to the renewal date. We sit down, feeling confident that we've got time to secure the deal. But here's the reality: this is our first big mistake, and it's likely the moment we lose the deal. The renewal process shouldn't start when the contract is about to expire - it should have begun the day after the contract was signed.

That's where a strong customer success program comes in. By focusing on value and ensuring the customer feels supported throughout the contract's entire lifecycle, we avoid the last-minute scramble. Whether the customer decides to renew or not, it should never be a surprise. Regular check-ins, listening, and adapting to the customer's changing needs are what make the difference, ensuring both parties are clear on where the relationship stands well before that renewal date arrives.

In the end, whether the partnership continues or it's time to move in new directions, a proactive approach to customer success helps everyone make informed decisions early - without the stress of last-minute negotiations or unexpected surprises. Let's explore this in a little more detail.

Waiting Until Renewal is a Risk

Waiting until the last minute to think about renewal is like cramming for an exam the night before. You're trying to demonstrate value, highlight results, and strengthen a relationship all at once. But by that point, the customer has already formed their opinion on whether they want to stay or go. If their experience hasn't met expectations, trying to resolve everything at the eleventh hour won't be enough.

The reality is that by the time the contract is up for renewal, the customer already knows if they're happy or not. They've been thinking about it, even if they haven't said anything yet. That's why customer success needs to be an ongoing process, something that runs through the entire lifecycle of the contract. If we wait until the end to check in, we're already on the back foot.

Best Time to Start the Renewal Process

As already mentioned, the renewal process should start the day after the contract is signed. The customer success program should enable us to prove value, address concerns, and ensure the customer feels supported from the very start. By weaving customer success into the customer relationship, we're laying the groundwork for a smooth renewal process long before the end date comes around.

No Surprises at Renewal Time

Let's imagine that the renewal date arrives, and both you and the customer already know exactly where things stand. If there were issues along the way, you've worked together to resolve them as they came up. If the customer's needs shifted, you've been right there, adjusting your approach and continuing to deliver value. By the time you sit down to discuss the renewal, it's not a stressful conversation - it's just the next logical step in a relationship that's been nurtured from day one.

That's the power of a strong program. When the customer knows they're being listened to, when they can see that their success is your priority, the decision to renew is easy. It's not something you have to rush through at the last minute to save the deal - it's the result of months or years of consistent effort, building trust, and proving value.

Ongoing Customer Success

So, how do we make sure the renewal process isn't a mad dash at the end? It comes down to having a strong customer success program that's proactive, not reactive. You need to be in regular communication, checking that the customer's goals are being met and adjusting when needed. If you've been working consistently with them throughout the contract, there's no need for a last-minute scramble to prove your value.

Customer success is something that should be woven into every interaction. It's not something we throw together at the end as a way to keep the business. By starting early and staying consistent, we avoid those dreaded surprises at renewal time, and instead, we build a solid, long-term partnership.

In the end, the best way to secure a renewal is to make sure there are no surprises for anyone. If we've done the work throughout the contract, the renewal becomes an easy decision, not a stressful negotiation. It's about working smart from the beginning, not rushing to fix things at the last minute.

Conclusion

Choosing not to renew a contract doesn't always mean that something went wrong. Sometimes, it's simply the natural conclusion of a business relationship that has served its purpose well. Both the customer and the seller might find themselves asking, "Does this still make sense for us?" In some instances, the answer may be that it's time to walk away, and that's perfectly okay. However, in most cases, if we've done our job right, the outcome is likely to be a renewal.

When both parties approach this decision with respect and transparency, it will mean everyone feels good about the choices being made. If we've taken the time to maintain open communication, consistently deliver value, and truly listen to the customer's needs throughout the contract, we're setting the foundations for a successful renewal. And that helps us to look ahead with optimism, knowing we've made the right choice as a team.

Lesson 20: Customer Advocacy

When we talk about customer success, we're really focusing on creating a positive experience throughout the customer's journey. But let's take it a step further and explore the idea of **customer advocacy**. This is more than having customers who use our products or services - and who ultimately choose to renew their relationship with us. It's about developing genuine supporters of our brand who are enthusiastic about sharing their experiences with others.

Think about your personal life for a moment. Which brands would you genuinely support when asked? Personally, I wouldn't say I'm fiercely loyal to any one brand. I feel that things change too often to be wedded to any product or service for too long - except for Sky TV.

Despite not meeting my ambitious standards of customer success we've discussed in this book; Sky doesn't even reach out during my contract or near its end. Instead, I receive an email saying, "Thanks for being a customer for 12 years. Your last Sky TV cost was £x, and this time it will be £y. There's no need to contact us; we'll automatically take your new payment starting on the 27th of next month."

Naturally, the first thing I do is open an incognito browser, head to Sky's website, and search for the latest deals. If my renewal seems higher than what new customers are offered, I know it's time to pick up the phone.

It would be easy for me to switch to another provider. Yet, there's always a twinge of anxiety at renewal time. Even though there are other options available, I actually prefer Sky TV. It just works - and it works exceptionally well. Over the years, they've continually evolved their platform with new features to a point where I genuinely believe no one else can match them. Whenever I visit friends and family, I've tried their competitors, and while they're improving, none seem to reach the same level. In fact, isn't Sky's slogan "Believe in Better"? It speaks volumes.

That's why I've renewed my contract for 12 consecutive terms. Not always because the price is the best around or because I feel I'm getting a fair deal, but because the product is simply second to none. I am an advocate for Sky.

Why Advocacy Works

Let's explore the theory behind customer advocacy, especially in light of our previous conversation about Sky TV. At its core, customer advocacy is all about turning satisfied customers into passionate supporters of your brand.

In the context of our earlier lessons and this section, customer success sits central to everything needed to achieve customer advocacy. When companies focus on delivering real value and creating a positive experience throughout the customer journey, they're building advocacy. Satisfied customers naturally want to shout from the rooftops about their experiences. Well, in my world, I might tell a few people how great a business is!

Building trust and loyalty is another essential piece of the sales leadership puzzle. Customers need to feel confident in the brand they're supporting. As we've mentioned many times already through this book, trust is created through consistent communication, transparency, and a genuine commitment to meeting their needs. Take my experience with Sky TV, for instance. Even though there are some frustrations during the renewal process due to price, the reliability and quality of their service keeps me loyal.

Emotional connection plays a significant role, too. When customers have that strong bond with a brand, they're more likely to advocate for it. As I mentioned earlier, the quality of Sky's product and the overall user experience build a sense of loyalty, making me more inclined to stick with them, even when the renewal process feels a bit impersonal.

Customer advocacy also encourages open and welcomed feedback. This kind of engagement helps companies to make meaningful improvements that enhance the customer experience. For instance, whenever I've shared my concerns about renewal pricing, Sky has consistently been willing to adjust it when possible. This willingness shows they truly value long-term relationships, and me as a customer.

And let's not overlook the importance of community building. When customers become advocates, they often create a community around the brand. Just look at how I've mentioned Sky in this book! This community shares experiences, provides support, and sparks discussions that further enhance the brand's reputation. Advocacy creates a positive cycle: satisfied customers attract new ones, which helps solidify the brand's presence in the market.

Manufacturer and Distributor Advocacy

I'd like to shift our conversation back to a B2B context and share an example of a 30+ year partnership between a manufacturer and one of its distributors. This enduring relationship is a testament to ongoing customer success efforts, leading to the strongest form of customer advocacy I have ever seen. While I need to anonymise the companies involved, I hope to paint a vivid picture of how robust this relationship has been over the years and why I believe it will continue to grow for many more to come.

Let's turn our focus to microscopy - pardon the pun. The manufacturer we're discussing is a world leader in optical filters, specifically designed for microscopy applications in research and development. Hopefully, you have a picture in your mind of someone in a white lab coat, peering through a microscope, intently examining a sample on a slide. By using optical filters to manipulate the light, the user can highlight specific features or anomalies in the sample they're reviewing.

I won't get too scientific or graphic, but it's worth mentioning that these samples often include biopsies taken from patients during recent hospital examinations.

As technology has advanced, traditional microscopes have evolved into sophisticated automated scanning machines. These machines digitise physical slides, converting them into high-quality digital images for analysis. In this process, optical filters play a vital role. They are designed to allow specific wavelengths (or colours) of light to pass through while blocking others. This selectivity enhances particular features of the slide being scanned, leading to improved image quality and colour accuracy.

Now, you can see how choosing the right optical filters is essential for clearer, more detailed scans. The distributor in this relationship is fully committed to customer success - meaning they focus on whether the researchers can achieve the results they need. It's crucial they provide the very best products from the leading manufacturer. This creates a fantastic partnership: the manufacturer produces high-quality optical filters, the distributor helps researchers select the ideal filter for their specific applications, and as a result, the researchers can achieve remarkable success in their work.

Ultimately, this kind of collaboration is making a significant impact in the fight against diseases we all know and despise, like cancer.

Building a strong relationship between a manufacturer and distributor certainly doesn't happen overnight. It requires years of dedicated effort to establish trust between the two businesses, all with the ultimate goal of ensuring success for the researchers using their products. When I reflect on this relationship, several key factors stand out as the reasons behind its effectiveness. Interestingly, none of these factors alone would make much of a difference; it's the combination of each element that truly drives success.

Components for Success

It takes time, trust, and a genuine commitment to collaboration at this level. Both parties must be wholeheartedly focused on supporting the success of the researchers who rely on their products. Here are some key elements that I observed that demonstrate exceptional advocacy between these two companies, highlighting the numerous ways their partnership is interconnected:

Shared Vision and Goals: At the top level, it's all about alignment. The leaders from both the manufacturer and distributor come together regularly with a shared vision for the future. They're on the same page about their strategic goals, which means the partnership is built on mutual commitment to long-term growth and success. This shared understanding opens the door for collaboration on everything from market strategies to product innovation.

Open Lines of Communication: Effective communication is vital at all levels of this partnership – from market strategy to daily deliveries. The team have regular meetings (typically weekly) and it's the open discussions that create a space where both teams can share insights, challenges, and opportunities. This dialogue allows for proactive problem-solving, which in my mind really does reinforce their commitment to each other and, more importantly, to the researchers they serve.

Empowering Teams Through Training: In an industry that's evolving so rapidly, keeping up with the latest methodologies and technologies is crucial. That's why the manufacturer consistently provides training for the distributor's team, ensuring they have the most up-to-date insights to support the end-user researchers effectively. From informative white papers to interactive workshops and even on-site visits to see manufacturing processes in action, these initiatives keep the team well-informed and engaged. As we've discussed, this commitment to training directly translates into better service for the researchers, building the advocacy that benefits everyone involved.

Collaborative Development: With the distributor's team engaging with a diverse range of researchers facing various challenges, there's a fantastic opportunity for product development. The manufacturer and distributor collaborate closely to create products and solutions that address the latest needs of these researchers. This strengthens their relationship of course, but it also reflects their shared commitment to ensuring that end users receive the best solutions. There's a brilliant sense of satisfaction across the team when researchers achieve new and transformational results, knowing that these successes are directly linked to the dedicated efforts in product development.

Welcoming Feedback: Whether feedback is brilliant or mediocre, good, or bad, it all holds value in this relationship. The manufacturer actively seeks input from the distributor about their experiences in the field. This feedback allows them to refine products and address any issues, demonstrating their genuine care for the distributor's success and, ultimately, for those fantastic researchers.

The Moral of This Story

Now, the two examples I've described here are quite different. I want to be clear that I'm not placing them on the same pedestal - far from it.

Take me, for instance, sitting comfortably on my sofa, thrilled every time I turn on the TV, knowing that the solution I'm using just works. I appreciate that Sky has invested time in developing something that delights its customers. Whether I see that effort or not, what truly matters is that I'm getting the results I expect.

Now, think about that researcher striving to find a cure for a dreaded disease. They aren't privy to all the behind-the-scenes work between the manufacturer and its distributor. They don't see the weekly calls, the training sessions, or the frantic efforts to ensure that essential materials are delivered promptly for an urgent project. All they notice is the high-quality solution that helps them achieve the results they expect.

Conclusion

So, what's the takeaway from these stories for you? I hope I've illustrated that regardless of your industry, application, or customer base, customer advocacy is in your hands. It's up to you to create that advocacy in a way that resonates with your business and your customers.

Focus on providing genuine value, and you'll naturally develop meaningful relationships that benefit both your customers and your brand. In the end, customer advocacy blossoms when you exceed expectations, building a loyalty that can last for years to come.

THE 'ONE GOLDEN RULE'

Lesson 21: Continuous Improvement Everywhere

The final piece of the sales leadership puzzle - the 'one golden rule' I live by - is Continuous Improvement Everywhere. Throughout this book, I've tried to offer insights into how you can improve your sales team, processes, and systems to achieve better results. But much like training muscles at the gym, servicing a car, or maintaining a diet, these improvements require constant refinement and optimisation. If you've ever learned to play a musical instrument, can you remember the first time you picked it up? It probably sounded awful, right? But with practice, running up and down the scales over and over, you began to improve.

I recall when my sister was learning to play the clarinet as a child. Our mum patiently waited for the day when the endless scales would give way to actual music. The music eventually came, but the scales never stopped. The reason? Those endless repetitions and tiny refinements were the key to her overall performance. And that's the point - practice is vital.

When you think about it, practice plays a huge role in any performance - be it music or sports. But how often do we take the time to "practice" in sales or sales leadership? How often do we allow ourselves the space to work on those tiny improvements that can make all the difference in our own performance?

Let me share a story about one of my greatest passions: Formula 1 racing. Strangely, I don't enjoy going to the racetrack itself. I find it more enjoyable to follow the sport on TV, where you can get a complete picture of the action. It's probably another reason why I've maintained my Sky TV subscription for so long, as I mentioned in the last chapter! To the uninitiated, Formula 1 might look like 20 overpaid drivers parading around a track for 90 minutes before celebrating with champagne. But for those of us who deeply appreciate the sport, the fascination lies in what happens behind the scenes - the preparation, the practice, and the endless pursuit of improvement.

Consider this for a moment: for every minute, a driver spends on the track during a Sunday race, they've probably spent 20 or 30 times that amount practising and preparing. As soon as the champagne is sprayed and the race is over, the work for the next race begins, which sometimes happens as soon as the following weekend.

On Monday morning, the drivers are back with their teams, analysing every detail from yesterday's race. What insights can they glean to apply to the next one? That week, the drivers spend hours in the gym, managing hydration, planning meals, and making sure they get adequate rest. Then they hit the simulators - doing hundreds of virtual laps of the next track, learning every straight and corner with precise accuracy. They simulate every possible scenario: high fuel loads, low fuel loads, soft tyres, hard tyres, wet conditions, dry conditions. Every detail is scrutinised.

By the time Friday arrives, it's time for the first practice session on the actual track - what's called Free Practice 1. This is the first time the driver gets to test the car on the circuit for that race. And while they've already spent countless hours in the simulator, nothing beats the real thing. The team gathers mountains of data from the car and the driver, analysing every aspect to optimise the car's aerodynamics, power, and efficiency.

But it's not just about the car. The driver too has to reflect on what they've learned from the virtual sessions. How does the car feel under race conditions? How is their body holding up under the extreme g-forces they're subjected to? The practice continues, with Free Practice 2 on Friday afternoon and Free Practice 3 on Saturday morning, followed by a break for more analysis and fine-tuning.

Then comes the crucial part of the weekend: qualifying. For those unfamiliar with the sport, qualifying consists of three rounds, with the five slowest drivers being eliminated in each of the first two rounds, leaving the fastest ten to battle it out for pole position in the final session. This is where continuous improvement truly pays off. The fastest driver earns the pole position, and the rest line up behind them on the grid based on their lap times.

On race day, while the teams are limited in the adjustments they can make to the car before the race begins due to regulations, they still work on optimising the car's performance within the allowable limits. The drivers, meanwhile, have the chance to do a few "reconnaissance laps" before the race starts. During these laps, they practise their start procedures and prepare the car for the critical moments when the lights go green. Even as they line up on the grid, the engineers are making last-minute tweaks, and the drivers undergo final mindset coaching, reaction tests, and hydration. (I imagine they squeeze in a quick trip to the loo as well!)

After the formalities of the national anthem, photos with A-list celebrities, and getting strapped into the car, it's just the driver and the machine. The race engineer might provide a few final instructions over the radio, but typically, it's silent. Why the quiet? Because at this moment, the only thing standing between the driver and a successful race is their skill and mindset. And that doesn't just materialise when the lights change from red to green. No, the success of that start, the first corner, the overtakes, the pit stops, the defence against being overtaken - all of it was set in motion the previous Monday.

But it's more than that. Every race is an opportunity to build upon the insights gained from every practice, every qualifying session, and every race that came before. The continuous improvement never stops. It's embedded in every detail, every moment, and every decision.

Practice for Sales Leadership

Hopefully, by now, the message is clear: success doesn't just happen by chance. While luck can sometimes play a role, more often than not, it's the relentless pursuit of improvement that separates the good from the great. Continuous practice, review, and refinement are essential. Just as a Formula 1 driver or a musician running scales works tirelessly for those marginal gains, so too must sales teams and leaders continually seek small adjustments that, over time, yield meaningful results.

Let's imagine two individuals: the first is Lewis Hamilton, arguably the greatest Formula 1 driver of all time (message me if you don't agree!). He's sitting at the front of the grid, waiting for the lights to turn green. The second is Tarquin Hughes, Key Account Manager at Acme Plc, waiting in the reception area of a client's office, about to meet the new purchasing manager. Now, compare how much practice and preparation Lewis has put into the engagement with that first corner, versus how much Tarquin has put into his first meeting with the customer. The contrast is stark, isn't it?

While Formula 1 and sales meetings are vastly different, the underlying principles remain the same. If Tarquin dedicated more time to practice – testing different scenarios, listening to best practices, seeking feedback on his performance, making sure he's equipped with all the right data, and ensuring he's in peak condition for high-performance – he would undoubtedly have a better outcome in his meeting.

So, what's the real issue here? In Lewis's world, his team creates endless opportunities for continuous improvement throughout the week. But in Tarquin's company, the focus is so heavily on the 'race' – the big meetings and the deals – that they overlook the critical importance of preparation. They miss that it's the groundwork, the practice, which leads to crossing the finish line first.

As sales leaders, it's our responsibility to create these opportunities for our teams. We must help them practice, refine, and continuously improve their performance. After all, what's good for Lewis Hamilton is good for our teams too.

So, let's explore some of the ways continuous improvement can be woven into your week to help both you and your teams achieve better results.

It Starts with You

As a sales leader, improving your own performance is just as important as helping your team grow. One of the best things you can do is take time for a bit of self-reflection. At the end of each week, just pause and ask yourself: how did things go? Were there decisions that really paid off, or were there moments where things didn't go as planned? Did you manage to spend time actively coaching your team, or did the week get taken over by firefighting? By being kind to yourself and honestly reviewing these areas, you'll start to see those little tweaks that can lead to even better results.

This time of reflection is also a terrific opportunity to check in on the bigger picture. Remember those three critical questions we talked about in Lesson 1?

Where are we now?

Where do we want to get to?

How are we going to get there?

I find that using this framework helps to keep everything aligned with your overall goals and objectives. It's a simple way to guide your thinking and ensure that you stay focused as you approach the week ahead.

Another useful approach is to ask for feedback from those around you. It's easy to get caught up in our routines, but sometimes a fresh perspective can really help. Whether it's from a mentor or a colleague, others might spot something you've missed or suggest small changes that could make a difference. I know it's not always easy to open up to feedback, but doing so can really accelerate your growth and help you find new ways to lead your team effectively.

Lastly, it's always a good idea to stay curious and keep learning. The sales world is constantly evolving, and there's always something new to discover. Whether it's reading up on the latest trends, attending a webinar, or simply keeping your ear to the ground, staying informed will help you keep your team on the right path. It doesn't have to be a big-time commitment, but these small efforts can go a long way.

Why not start this practice now? Set aside just one hour at the end of each week for self-reflection and make it a recurring session in your diary. Throughout the week, jot down any notes and ideas that come to mind, so you have something to refer back to during this dedicated time. When that hour rolls around, use it positively to help you move forward. Focus on what went well and where you can improve but try to avoid negativity that might weigh you down. The purpose of this session is to prepare yourself for success in the week ahead.

Weekly Team Talk

One of the best ways to cement that marketing and sales alignment we talked about earlier is through a weekly team talk. It's a chance for everyone to discuss the strategies, tactics, and challenges that the team is working through. In one of my previous companies, we called this the Weekly MASH. MASH stood for Marketing and Sales Huddle, and the word 'huddle' was quite fitting because that's exactly what it was. There wasn't a formal meeting room or a long agenda, just a quick and effective gathering.

Every Wednesday morning at 10 am, the marketing and sales teams would gather in a central spot in the open office, with an open mind, and a positive attitude, ready to talk about continuous improvement.

These sessions were co-led by me, as the Sales Director, and the Marketing Director. We'd start with a quick review of my favourite set of questions:

Where are we now?

Where do we want to get to?

How are we going to get there?

This was our chance to review the progress of our current strategy, often by looking at the numbers, while also highlighting key successes and addressing strategic challenges. It gave everyone a clear view of what was working and where we needed to focus our attention.

Once we had that guiding direction, we'd move on to discuss the key marketing activities for the coming week, any major client meetings, potential blockers, ongoing initiatives, and any team coaching or training plans. It was all about teamwork, problem-solving, and keeping the momentum going.

One thing that really helped with these huddles was a simple ideas board. Throughout the week, anyone could jot down continuous improvement ideas on a Post-It-Note and stick it on the board. During the MASH, we'd review the ideas as a group, discussing which ones were viable. If an idea had potential, we'd log it with an action owner and track the progress each week. The really promising ones would go into a more formal initiatives strategy document for deeper exploration with the senior team.

It's such a simple way to get started. No long meetings, no complex processes – just a chance to bring everyone together, make sure the whole team has a voice, and keep the continuous improvement journey alive. It's a small commitment, but it makes a big difference in aligning your teams and driving results.

Lean Principles for Sales Improvement

At another company I worked for, famous for its approach to lean manufacturing, those key principles also extended to the office environment. For sales, this meant a daily stand-up meeting with the front-line team, including our marketing colleagues. The focus remained on sales results, but there was a clear recognition that the overall company processes played a crucial role in supporting commercial efforts.

Much like the weekly MASH, this daily meeting was a quick team huddle in the office, and it was known as the Daily QDIPS. This approach helped align everyone, ensuring that sales, marketing, and operations were all on the same page, addressing challenges as they arose, and contributing to continuous improvement efforts across the board.

QDIPS is a tool used in Lean and Six Sigma methodologies to drive continuous improvement and problem-solving in business processes. It stands for:

Quality – **D**elivery – **I**nventory – **P**roductivity - **S**afety

Let's break each one down.

Quality: In sales, quality often refers to the accuracy and professionalism in communication with customers, the quality of leads, or the thoroughness of proposals.

Example: The team might notice that several deals were lost due to incomplete or poorly tailored proposals. To resolve this, they could establish a review process to ensure that every proposal meets exacting standards before being sent to clients. This could include having another team member review proposals for clarity, accuracy, and alignment with the client's needs.

Delivery: Delivery in a sales context could refer to the timely execution of client meetings, follow-ups, or meeting proposal deadlines.

Example: If clients are frequently receiving proposals or follow-ups late, this could lead to missed opportunities. In this instance, the team can implement tighter internal deadlines, making sure that proposals are submitted within a set time limit after meetings. Additionally, automating reminders for follow-ups can ensure that no client is left waiting for a response.

Inventory: While inventory is typically thought of in manufacturing, in sales it can refer to the availability of marketing materials, demo products, or even leads in the pipeline.

Example: If a sales team is short on product demo kit or brochures to highlight to clients, it can really slow down the sales process. Without the right materials, it's difficult to present the product effectively and can leave clients with unanswered questions. To tackle this, the team can make sure they always have an adequate supply of the sales tools required.

Productivity: Productivity in sales can be measured in terms of the number of calls made, meetings held, or proposals sent per day, week, or month.

Example: If a sales manager notices that team members are spending too much time on administrative tasks instead of selling, a focus on productivity might lead to adopting some tasks in the CRM system, freeing up more time for direct client engagement and revenue-generating activities.

Safety: In a sales team, Safety might not refer to physical hazards but rather emotional or mental well-being. It could involve creating a supportive work environment where salespeople feel comfortable sharing challenges without fear of judgment.

Example: A high-pressure sales environment might lead to

burnout. Working together, the team could implement regular check-ins to ensure that everyone is managing their workload well. creating an environment where it's okay to ask for help.

Advanced Continuous Improvement

It's likely that the ideas I've shared for getting started with continuous improvement will be more than enough to get things rolling. But if you're already on top of those basics and seeing good results, you might want to consider stepping things up a notch. When continuous improvement becomes ingrained across an organisation, not just in sales leadership, the potential for team collaboration grows exponentially.

At one company I worked for, continuous improvement was done on an industrial scale. Every department, and even sub-departments, had their own continuous improvement work cells, each with boards highlighting everything from major strategy developments to small team tweaks. Each week, the senior executive team would tour the building, visiting these work cells to stay updated on the latest initiatives. The leaders from each work cell reported to a programme management office, ensuring that projects were delivered on time, within budget, and implemented with a project management mindset. The pace of change was like nothing I'd experienced before – and I haven't seen anything like it since at that scale.

To encourage and reward these efforts, the company introduced STAR Awards – Special Thanks and Recognition. Each month, a bronze award was given to the best ideas in every main department, with a silver award for the overall winner. And once a year, gold awards were presented for the most impactful ideas across the business.

After a couple of years, the entire 100-metre corridor of the facility was lined with framed awards, recognising those who had gone beyond with their continuous improvement contributions.

This is the beauty of continuous improvement – it can be as simple as a one-hour reflection session, a weekly team huddle, a daily stand-up, or it can evolve into a full organisational culture. Whatever approach works for you and your team, it's the commitment to keep moving forward that really counts.

Further Reading

There are so many tools and resources available to support your continuous improvement journey in sales leadership, and I'd love to share a few that I've personally found helpful. Here's a starting point for your further research, moving from easier concepts – as I see them - to more advanced techniques:

Key Performance Indicator Tracking: Establishing and monitoring KPI's to measure progress and success in specific areas.

Performance Reviews: Regular assessments of individual and team performance that focus on growth and areas for improvement.

Brainstorming Sessions: Collaborative meetings aimed at generating a wide range of ideas and solutions to challenges faced by the team.

Continuous Feedback Loops: Establishing mechanisms for ongoing feedback from team members and clients to identify areas for improvement in real-time.

SWOT Analysis: A strategic planning tool that helps teams assess their internal and external environment through Strengths, Weaknesses Opportunities, and Threats.

Plan–Do–Check-Act: A cyclical model for continuous improvement that encourages teams to plan changes, implement them, assess the results, and refine the process.

Fishbone Diagram (Ishikawa): A visual tool used to identify potential causes of a problem, allowing teams to explore a range of factors contributing to an issue.

5 Whys: A simple yet effective technique for exploring the cause-and-effect relationships underlying a particular problem by repeatedly asking "why" to dig deeper.

3Cs (Concern, Cause, Countermeasure): A problem-solving tool that helps teams identify concerns, explore root causes, and develop countermeasures.

Root Cause Analysis (RCA): A method used to identify the fundamental cause of a problem, ensuring that solutions address the core issue rather than just symptoms.

A3 Thinking: A structured approach to problem-solving that fits on an A3-sized sheet, promoting clarity and conciseness in presenting issues and solutions.

Value Stream Mapping: A visual tool that helps teams identify and analyse the flow of materials and information needed to bring a product or service to the customer.

Kaizen: A philosophy of continuous improvement focused on small, incremental changes that lead to significant enhancements over time.

Lean Six Sigma: A methodology that combines lean manufacturing principles with Six Sigma techniques to improve process efficiency and reduce variation.

Hoshin Kanri: A strategic planning process that aligns goals and objectives across all levels of an organisation, ensuring everyone is working toward the same vision.

Some Final Thoughts

Have you ever heard that phrase: "The best time to plant a tree was 20 years ago. The second-best time is now"? It's a saying that resonates deeply in many aspects of life, including our professional journeys. When it comes to continuous improvement, the best time to start was probably 20 "months" ago, but when is the second-best time? I'll let you decide.

Conclusion

So, there you have it – the 'one golden rule': Continuous Improvement Everywhere. It's more than just a motto; it's a mindset. It's about committing to always strive for better, learning from every experience, and using those lessons to increase performance. Whether you're leading a sales team or preparing for the next Formula 1 race, the key to long-term success is never being satisfied with "good enough." There's always something to improve, and the journey towards excellence never truly ends.

Good luck on your sales leadership journey, and if you ever need support, feel free to look me up on LinkedIn. I'd be more than happy to help.

Acknowledgements

Without the expert guidance of remarkable individuals throughout my career, I wouldn't have gained the insights that form the foundation of this book. I am grateful to all my colleagues, mentors, coaches, and leaders who have contributed in many ways.

I also want to thank Nate Lansdell of A Smile A Day Photography for beautifully capturing my emotions in the book's cover photo.

A special thanks to my sister Denise and her husband David for their patience during the final editing phases of the book. I deeply appreciate all the effort you put in.

Finally, to my wife Karen and daughter Harriet, your unwavering support means everything to me, and I am forever grateful for your love.

Printed in Great Britain
by Amazon

50986928R00116